LOST SKI AREAS
— of —
Southern Vermont

Southern Vermont was once filled with more ski areas than today's skiers can ever imagine. Sixty ski areas once operated in addition to the thirteen that remain in operation today. Once known to generations of skiers, areas like Dutch Hill, Snow Valley and Hogback are slowly fading away into history. Many skiers once collected patches such as these after they had skied these smaller areas in southern Vermont. *Courtesy Woodward Bousquet.*

LOST SKI AREAS

of

Southern Vermont

JEREMY K. DAVIS

THE
History
PRESS

Published by The History Press
Charleston, SC 29403
www.historypress.net

*Cover images courtesy of Woodward Bousquet, Ellen Howard, Chris Lundquist and the New England
Ski Museum.*

All images are courtesy of the author unless otherwise noted.

First published 2010
Second printing 2011
Third printing 2012
Fourth printing 2013

Manufactured in the United States

ISBN 978.1.59629.871.2

Davis, Jeremy K.
Lost ski areas of southern Vermont / Jeremy K. Davis.
p. cm.
ISBN 978-1-59629-871-2
1. Ski resorts--Vermont--History. 2. Ski resorts--Vermont--History--Pictorial works. 3. Skis
and skiing--Vermont--History. 4. Skis and skiing--Vermont--History--Pictorial works. 5.
Vermont--History, Local. 6. Vermont--History, Local--Pictorial works. I. Title.
GV854.5.V5D38 2010
796.9309743--dc22
2010021954

CONTENTS

CONTENTS

ACKNOWLEDGEMENTS

There are many people to thank for their assistance in the creation of this book. Skiing enthusiasts contributed vintage and contemporary imagery, personal accounts of ski areas, historical guidebooks and articles. Former operators of these lost areas and their families provided invaluable descriptions from firsthand accounts.

Vintage and contemporary imagery was submitted or obtained from organizations including the New England Ski Museum, the Vermont Ski Museum, Friends of Woodstock Winters, the Marlboro Historical Society, the Putney School and the UNH Digital Collections.

Imagery was also contributed from the following ski history enthusiasts, ski area operators and their families: Tom Barbera, Anne Marie Blackman, Woodward Bousquet, Don Cosgrove, Bill Currier, David Dematteis, Kathe Dillman, Ryan Grace, Tom Hildreth, John Hitchcock, Dick Hogarth, Ellen Howard, Tim Ingalls, Bill Jenkins, James Jennings, Nancy Leavy, Paul Lemieux, Karen Lorentz, Chris Lundquist, Hope McLaughlin, Duncan McNeill, Joe Morein, Laurie Puliafico, Doug Riley, Dan Robertson, Ted Russell, Koke Twigg-Smith and Brian Wyckoff.

Ryan Grace and Betsy McDonough Brown were very helpful following up on leads and exploring some of these areas with the author in 2009 and 2010. Dan Robertson's visits to and photographs of some of these areas were also appreciated.

The history of Hogback Mountain could not have been completed without the help of Forrest Holzapfel of the Marlboro Historical Society, Dick and Marcia Hamilton, Ruth and Sally White and Bob and Nancy Anderson of the Hogback Mountain Conservation Association.

ACKNOWLEDGEMENTS

The history of Snow Valley could not have been completed without the help of Rick Birmingham, Kathe Dillman, Buzz Eichel, Clark Comollo and Chris Parker.

Jonathan Robinson was instrumental with his assistance regarding Woodstock areas, as well as a few other lost areas. Sherman Howe of Friends of Woodstock Winters also provided great assistance in these areas.

Bill Jenkins was an enormous help on many of these areas and provided imagery and commentary that was invaluable. Areas like Hogback and Green Mountain College would be scarcely depicted if not for him.

Koke Twigg-Smith and his family helped bring to life Sonnenberg and the anniversary of the Woodstock Ski Tow with photographs.

Joe Parks, former owner of Prospect Mountain, was very helpful with the overall history of that ski area.

John Hitchcock, a ski writer for sixty years, provided one-of-a-kind photographs of Dutch Hill, and his inside knowledge of some of these areas was appreciated.

Thanks to Jeff Leich at the New England Ski Museum and Meredith Scott at the Vermont Ski Museum for their assistance in obtaining unique vintage imagery.

Author Karen Lorentz was very helpful regarding lost ski areas in the Rutland vicinity and provided a unique map of Shrewsbury Ski Area.

For every person who has supported www.nelsap.org over the years, I can not begin to say what that has meant to me regarding our goal of documenting and preserving every lost ski area in New England.

Finally, a special thank-you to my parents, Ken and Linda Davis, and my brother, Nathan, and his wife, Stephanie, for supporting my ski history research over the years and to Scott Drake, who encourages and supports me every day!

Any omissions in the above are deeply regretted.

INTRODUCTION

Southern Vermont has a rich and diverse ski history. Amazingly, seventy-four ski areas have operated in the region. Today, just fourteen ski areas remain lift-served and open, though a few of those are not open to the public. Why did so many ski areas close? What happened to cause the loss of so many areas?

The reasons are many—overinvestment, poor snowmaking, local competition, widely variable weather from season to season, changing skier habits, insurance costs and sometimes just plain bad luck. Each lost ski area experienced at least one of these, and some experienced all of them.

A lost ski area is defined as a ski area that once offered lift-served and organized skiing. The lifts can range from simple rope tows to double chairlifts. The size of the area or the number of lifts is not important. Trails that were never accessible by lift, while important in some cases, are not included here. An area becomes "lost" once it is closed for good and the area is abandoned for skiing. A lost ski area rarely reopens, but this has occurred a few times.

Almost all of these lost areas are remembered quite positively by those who owned, operated and skied at them. Many learned to ski on their family-friendly slopes. Families watched their children grow up at them, and some skiers met their future spouses here. The remaining larger ski areas of today offer some incredible skiing, but most lack the intimate, local feel of these lost ski areas.

Many of these lost areas have become so overgrown with trees that they are no longer skiable, even by those hearty enough to hike to the top. A few, though, including Hogback and Dutch Hill, have some skiable lines and no trespassing concerns. Many of the others, though, are located on private land—if you choose to explore or backcountry ski a lost area, be sure to seek permission from the landowner first. Areas specifically mentioned as "private property" in the captions should definitely be avoided, but some can be viewed from a road or from a distance.

This book will focus on Vermont's four southernmost counties and will examine the wide variety of ski areas that once were operational. The tour begins in Windsor County—where lift-served ski areas were first established—moves west to Rutland County and then south to Bennington County and east to Windsor County. Hybrid ski areas, areas that don't quite fit into being completely lost to the public, have their own chapter, followed by the few small ski areas that remain in operation. Areas are listed alphabetically, except for Windsor County, where the first lift-served ski area is featured first.

Chapter 1
LOST SKI AREAS OF WINDSOR COUNTY

O ur tour of lost ski areas begins in Windsor County. With only twelve known lost ski areas, it is tied with Bennington County for the least number in all of Vermont's southern four counties. The vast majority of lost areas within the county were small rope tow ski areas, with a few exceptions.

Windsor County was home to several important lost ski areas, including the first lift-served skiing in southern Vermont and New England. It all began at Clinton Gilbert's farm in Woodstock, where the first rope tow began operation on January 23, 1934. The following winters, rope tows began sprouting up across the county and all over New England.

Three ski areas remain fully in operation today, including Mount Ascutney, Suicide Six, Quechee Lakes, Hill and Okemo. Mount Ascutney was briefly on the lost list from 1991 to 1993 but never seriously degenerated and has been in continuous operation ever since.

Additional ski areas not pictured include:

Altow/Cemetery Hill Ski Area, Norwich: Located in Norwich, this ski area was started by Al Peavey in the late 1940s and was later owned by Fred Briggs and Elwin Phillips in the early 1950s. Later, it was named Cemetery Hill due to an adjacent cemeterey that now occupies the former slope. Betsy Snite, future Olympic slalom silver medalist, learned to ski here.

Black River High School, Ludlow: A rope tow operated behind the high school in the late 1940s into the 1950s and was popular with local students.

Burrington Hill, Windsor: Located two miles north of town on Route 5, this area had a long rope tow, nighttime skiing and tobogganing in the late 1930s and early 1940s. It was owned by F.C. Burrington. This was not the Burrington Hill in Windham County.

Frederick Webster Tow, South Pomfret: Frederick Webster operated a (mainly) privately used eight-hundred-foot rope tow at his home in South Pomfret in the mid-1970s.

Hartford School District, White River Junction: The school district operated two short rope tows for students in the mid-1970s behind the high school.

Lundhugel, West Hartford: Open in the later 1930s and early 1940s, this ski area offered a clubhouse and two rope tows.

Okemo Outing Club, Ludlow: According to Karen Lorentz, author of *Okemo: All Come Home*, this rope tow operated in the late 1930s on the Walter Slack farm. The lift was removed in 1943.

Prosper Ski Tow: Rupert Lewis operated a couple of rope tows and a jump at his farm in South Pomfret in the late 1930s and early 1940s.

THE WHITE CUPBOARD SKI WAY AND WOODSTOCK SKI HILL

Woodstock, Vermont, has the distinction of hosting the first rope tow to ever operate in the United States. It was the place where the modern concept of a ski lift, lessons and affiliated lodging all came together. The first rope tow had been invented and installed in Shawbridge, Quebec, by Alexander Foster in 1932. On the New Year's weekend of 1934, skiers Douglas Burden, Tom Gammack and Barklie Henry were staying at the White Cupboard Inn in Woodstock. They had done much skiing on Clinton Gilbert's farm just north of town and wanted to find an easier way to the top instead of hiking. They challenged innkeepers Bob and Betty Royce to have a rope tow built on Gilbert's Hill (pictured here in 1934), as they had heard of one operating in Quebec. *Courtesy Sherman Howe, Friends of Woodstock Winters.*

The three skiers contributed seventy-five dollars each to the Royces, who immediately went out to find someone who could construct a tow. Betty's brother, William Koch, recommended his friend, David Dodd, of Newbury, Vermont. Dodd was hired to assemble the rope tow on Gilbert's Hill, which the Royces had leased for ten dollars for the rest of the season. Dodd gathered all of the equipment for the tow and, amazingly, built it in just a few weeks. Gus Buckman at the Billings Farm spliced the rope, and the ski area sold its first ticket on January 28, 1934. The White Cupboard Ski-Way, the first lift-served ski area in New England, was now open! The following week, members of the Boston-based Hochgebirge Ski Club arrived, and news of the lift spread like wildfire. *Courtesy Sherman Howe, Friends of Woodstock Winters.*

The first rope tow certainly had problems, as it was a prototype, including its engine needing to be replaced twice. The following year, Bunny Bertram secured the lease on Gilbert's Hill before the Royces (who had a falling out with Gilbert over their low lease) by offering Gilbert more of a share of the ticket sales. Bertram changed the name of the ski area to the Woodstock Ski Tow, and it ran during the 1934–35 season. The following year, Gilbert moved on to the Gully and then to Suicide Six, though the Woodstock Ski Tow continued to operate. *Courtesy Sherman Howe, Friends of Woodstock Winters.*

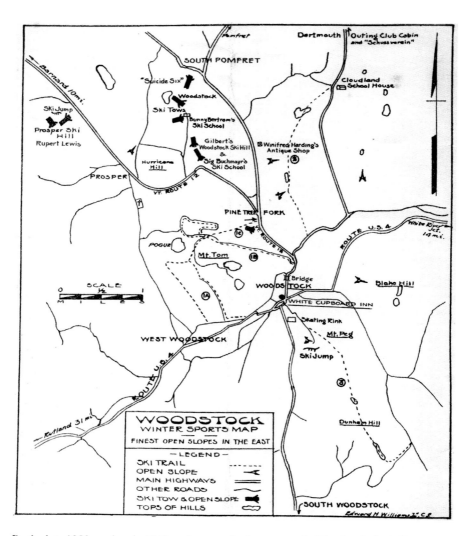

By the late 1930s and early 1940s, other tows had sprung up in Woodstock, including at the Gully, Prosper Hill, Mount Tom and Suicide Six. Competition was fierce, as were rival ski schools. In this 1939–40 map, Sig Buchmayr's Ski School operated at the Woodstock Ski Hill, with Bunny Bertram's at the Gully. Woodstock Ski Hill continued to operate until the late 1940s or early 1950s and then faded away. *Courtesy New England Ski Museum.*

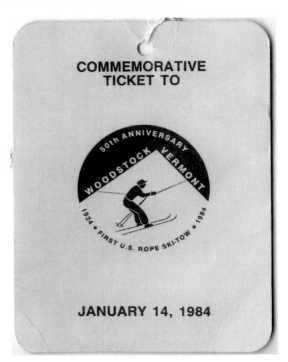

On January 14, 1984, a fiftieth anniversary celebration was held to commemorate the opening of the first rope tow in the United States. This oak tag ticket harkened back to the type of tickets that ski areas originally used, unlike today's sticky-back or scannable tickets. *Courtesy New England Ski Museum/Bill Currier.*

Bill Alsup from Poma lifts was in charge of the reconstruction of the rope tow, and he hired Bill Currier, a lift engineer and inspector, to construct a replica rope tow for the fiftieth anniversary celebration in 1984. Currier constructed this rope tow using a Model A Ford with a 1931 Phaeton engine from Koke Twigg-Smith. He took a sample ride on Friday, January 13, 1984, becoming the first person to ride a rope tow on this slope in about forty years. This certificate of appreciation was given to Currier in thanks for his hard work for the celebration. *Courtesy New England Ski Museum/ Bill Currier.*

Above: One of the events for the celebration included a race from the base of the original Gilbert's Hill to the top and then back down the other side and up to the top of nearby Suicide Six, followed by a race to the bottom of that ski area. Here, racers line up to load the replica rope tow. One can just make out the Model A Ford with a 1931 Phaeton engine at the far left. *Courtesy Koke Twigg-Smith.*

Left: Here, racers ride up the replica rope tow to begin the race. Note that some racers decided to hike to the top instead of riding the rope tow. *Courtesy Koke Twigg-Smith.*

Though the replica rope tow never operated again after that weekend, the towers still stand on the former Gilbert Farm. This 2010 view shows that the slope remains much the same as it has over its history. There is a historical marker at this location, just a few miles north of Woodstock on Route 12. One can reflect at this site on how lift-served skiing has changed from this humble rope tow into today's mega resorts.

CHESTER PINNACLE SKI AREA

The Chester Pinnacle Ski Area was a long-lasting, complete winter sports facility located in the town of Chester. It began operating in the late 1930s with a 1,500-foot-long rope tow and added another rope tow in the early 1940s. Ski jumping was available on a fifty-meter jump, with ice skating, tobogganing, cross-country skiing and more. Its easy access just outside of downtown provided residents with a convenient place to ski. By the 1960s, just one 700-foot rope tow was in operation, maintained by the Chester Outing Club and, later, the town. Pictured here is a view of the slope and rope tow in 1984. *Courtesy Tom Hildreth.*

The Pinnacle closed in 1989, becoming one of the last rope tow ski areas to do so in southern Vermont. While no longer offering skiing, the Chester Pinnacle remains an active place for outdoor recreation. A designated sledding area allows sliders to enjoy the former ski slope, while in the summer basketball courts, baseball diamonds, tennis courts and other facilities allow for outdoor sports. One can also explore the former ski area, located off Lover's Lane in Chester.

FUN VALLEY SKI AREA

SKI

FUN VALLEY

SOUTH ROYALTON
VERMONT

This twelve - hundred - foot tow carries you to the summit of a northeast slope, with a four - hundred - foot vertical drop. Twenty acres of open ski slopes offer terrain for all types of skiing. Thrills on our nose-dive trail. Here are slopes for the expert, intermediate and novice. Instructor available.

* * *

At the base: Lunches are served in the shelter, plus ample free parking space in full view of all activities.

* * *

Tow rates are one dollar ($1.00) per day.

* * *

Fun Valley is located one mile from the Railroad Station, on the road leading to the Joseph Smith Monument, one-eighth mile from the main highway, Route 14.

* * *

For reservations or information telephone 92-22, South Royalton, Vt., or write Terrace Lodge, Inc., Sharon, Vt. Here you will find rates that will please you and hospitality you will long remember. These accommodations are only a short distance from Fun Valley, with transportation available from Lodge to Ski Area.

* * *

You, your friends, your club will find fun for all at

FUN VALLEY

(Member of Central Vermont Ski Association)

Fun Valley Ski Area was located in South Royalton, on the northern edge of Windsor County. Owned and operated by Phil Trottier, who operated the Terrace Lodge, the ski area operated in the late 1940s and into the 1950s. It was essentially a semiprivate ski area for guests of the lodge, but other skiers were welcome. *Courtesy New England Ski Museum.*

MOUNT TOM

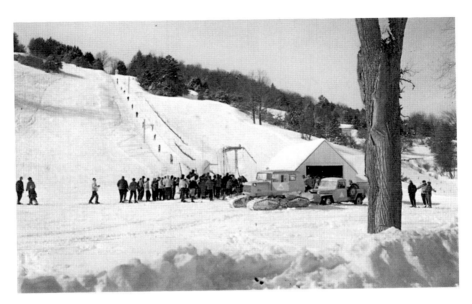

Mount Tom in Woodstock was used for downhill skiing from the mid-1930s until the late 1970s. It was conveniently located just one mile north of the village of Woodstock. In the mid-1930s, it was the location of Jim Parker's Ski School, who was an instructor at the White Cupboard Inn. At the inn, he had a shop in which ski equipment was sold. When his ski school opened, the area featured a rope tow and a broad slope. Skiing continued at Mount Tom in the 1940s and 1950s. In the early 1960s, the ski area operated with a baby Poma and this longer summit Pomalift. *Courtesy Laurie Puliafico.*

In the early 1960s, Mount Tom was purchased by RockResorts, owned by Laurance Rockefeller. Mount Tom was then tied into Suicide Six, which was also owned by Rockefeller. The two ski areas shared advertising and tickets and became known as Woodstock's Tom and Six. This 1968 brochure cover shows an artist's rendering of Mount Tom and the Pomalift. *Courtesy New England Ski Museum.*

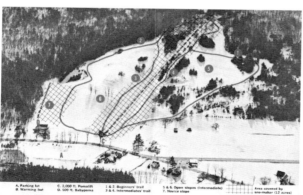

Mount Tom featured a vertical drop of just over four hundred feet and was geared to beginners, intermediates and families. The skiing was mostly on open slopes with scattered tree islands, though a few trails were available. A warming hut at the base served food. A small snowmaking system allowed for skiing during lean periods. In the mid- to late 1970s, Suicide Six was upgraded with new chairlifts and facilities, and it became impractical to continue running a smaller ski area just a few miles away. Mount Tom then closed in the late 1970s. *Courtesy New England Ski Museum.*

Today, Mount Tom is no longer used by skiers, but the open ski slope and trails are still visible. The area is accessible for hiking. The former Pomalift once ran from the middle right up through the gap in the trees at the summit. Almost no traces of skiing infrastructure, aside from the slopes and trails, are found today.

SPRINGFIELD

A community rope tow operated in Springfield, Vermont, beginning in the mid-1930s. Cal Coniff, who would later be the president of the National Ski Areas Association, as well as manage Mount Tom in Massachusetts, worked here as a youngster. During World War II, the factories in Springfield, Vermont, were running around the clock, and there was no excess labor to run the ski tow. Coniff volunteered to work at the ski area for no pay. The lift was a new, state-of-the-art Underwood Rope Tow with an electric drive at the top. When Coniff arrived, his job was to walk to the summit to start up the motor. In the fall, he would help clear the brush on the slopes with a friend of his. Bill Currier, a lift engineer, spliced the tow during its history. The ski area closed in the late 1970s but reopened in 1984 under the auspices of the Lions Club. Sadly, it only ran for a few more years, until 1988. By 2000, the slopes were already growing in, but the old rope tow was still standing.

Chapter 2
LOST SKI AREAS OF RUTLAND COUNTY

Rutland County is home to seventeen former ski areas. They run the full gamut from small community rope tows to much larger ski areas with multiple lifts. Early lost areas were small start-ups that closed during World War II. Later ski areas had to contend with strong competition from two much larger ski areas in the county, Killington and Pico, which continue to operate today.

Geographically, lost ski areas were found in two main belts—the Green Mountains in the eastern half of the county and the Taconics in the western half. Areas in the Taconics such as Birdseye and High Pond did not receive quite the amount of natural snow that fell in the higher elevations of the county at areas like Pico and Killington. Most of the lost areas in the Green Mountains were small rope tow areas, such as Dick's Tow or Shrewsbury Peak.

To help compete against their larger rivals, areas like Hyde Manor or Apple Hill offered lodging and other events. A few areas, such as Birdseye, were open for nighttime skiing, which was not offered at the larger resorts.

Additional ski areas not pictured include:

Burnham Hollow, Middletown Springs: According to John Williams, who was a member of the Burnham Hollow Ski Club, this rope tow was started and operated by Charles and Katie Colvin in the 1950s. Williams remembers that access came from a suspension bridge on the Poultney River.

Dick's Tow, Killington: According to Karen Lorentz, author of *Killington: A Story of Mountains and Men*, Richard Candlish built and operated Dick's Ski Tow near what is now the base of the Killington Access Road during the 1940s.

Maplewood Winter Sports Center, Fair Haven: Located on South Main Street, this ski area operated from the late 1930s into the early 1940s and featured a short rope tow and a toboggan chute.

Mountain Meadow Club, Sudbury: A 1948 map lists the Mountain Meadow Club as operating a rope tow, but little else is known.

Mountain Top Inn, Chittenden: The Mountain Top Inn operated a rope tow on a large hill above the inn on Mount Tronso in the 1950s. A T-bar lift area was later constructed at the inn, detailed in the captions in this chapter.

Proctor Rope Tow, Proctor: Operated by the Town of Proctor, this small ski area was open from the 1960s through 1974 and featured a wide slope, a narrow trail and an ice skating rink.

Rutland Junior College, Rutland: Rutland Junior College, now the College of St. Joseph, offered a short rope tow for students near its campus in the 1940s.

Rutland Recreation Rope Tow, Rutland: This small ski area was open from the late 1940s until 1976 at the Rutland Country Club.

Ski Haven, Killington: This rope tow ski area briefly operated during the late 1940s.

APPLE HILL SKI AREA

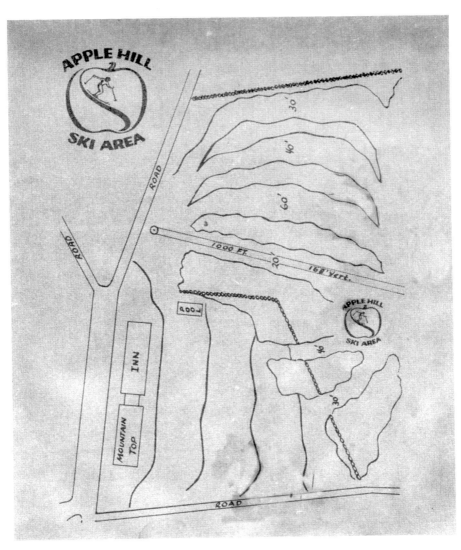

The Apple Hill Ski Area operated at the Mountain Top Inn in Chittenden from the 1960s through 1978 and was managed by Bill Wolfe. It was small, with a vertical drop of just 170 feet, and was mostly used by guests. It was an "upside down" ski area, where skiers could begin at the inn and ski down to the base on several trails, shown here in a 1970s trail map. A T-bar then provided access back to the summit. This T-bar was purchased by Wolfe from Abercrombie & Fitch in New York City, who operated it on a glacier.

After closing in 1978, Apple Hill was allowed to be reforested. Portions of the lift remain as of 2009, including the operator's hut and portions of the engine of the lift at the bottom of the ski area. One lift tower also remains midway on the lift line. While downhill skiing is no longer offered at Mountain Top, its Nordic Center offers top-notch cross-country skiing in spectacular surroundings. For more information, visit www.mountaintopinn.com.

BIRDSEYE MOUNTAIN SKI AREA

Birdseye Mountain Ski Area, located in Castleton, was founded by Bill Jenkins and investors in 1961. The plans for Birdseye originally called for a summer operation named the Vermont Mountain Park, focusing on Vermont life and history, along with facilities at the summit. The winter operations were to come later; however, it was decided to begin the ski area portion first. The Vermont Mountain Park was never built. Two Stabil Disc lifts were built at Birdseye in the early 1960s, along with lower trails. This 1963 view of the ski area from what is now Route 4A shows the lower slopes and access road. *Courtesy Bill Jenkins.*

Above: Stabil Disc lifts were a unique type of ski lift that Bill Jenkins and Stan Whitney installed at Birdseye and at a few other ski areas in New England. They are similar to Platterpull lifts, where skiers would ride up the mountain on a disc attached to a gravity retraction system with rubber tubing. It was comfortable and flexible to ride and was safer than other Platterpull or Pomalifts at that time. Here, skiers ride one of the lifts on the main slope. The western exposure and lower elevation often resulted in spring-like conditions, where employees would have to shovel snow onto the lift track. *Courtesy Bill Jenkins.*

Opposite top: Another view of main slope shows the lower section of the Stabil Disc lift along with the base lodge and parking lot. The lift is still standing as of 2010, nearly fifty years after it was installed. By 2010, the parking lot area had totally reverted to marshland. The base lodge was later expanded, with a second floor added onto it. To the north of this main slope was the beginner's rope tow and further north, a thirty-meter jump. *Courtesy Bill Jenkins.*

Opposite bottom: The second Stabil Disc lift was installed on the north side of Birdseye and served several slopes and trails. This summer photo shows Stan Whitney's wife and daughter testing out the lift, with the main slope and other Stabil Disc lift in the background. The two-person attachment was never used, but if it had been, it would have been the only kind in New England. Note the carpet-like smoothness of the slope, along with snowmaking pipelines along the liftline. Birdseye offered some of Vermont's earliest snowmaking on the main slope, utilizing twelve Larchmont snow guns. *Courtesy Bill Jenkins.*

The bullwheel of the north-facing Disc lift is shown here, newly constructed in 1963. The lift ended just below a major power line, which was built shortly after the property for Birdseye was constructed. Original plans to add a chairlift beginning near the top of this Disc lift to the summit did not come to pass. Had it been constructed, it would have needed to run through a tunnel under the power lines—which would have been a first for Vermont and New England! *Courtesy Bill Jenkins.*

Above: Besides the other Disc lifts, a gentle two-hundred-foot-long rope tow allowed many young skiers to learn in a safe environment. Quite a few Rutland- and Castleton-area kids learned to ski here, and many of their parents were able to watch them easily from the base of the tow. *Courtesy Bill Jenkins.*

Right: Nighttime skiing was a popular activity at Birdseye, which had one of the new such operations in the state. Birdseye was closed most weekdays but did offer nighttime skiing on Thursday and Friday nights for just two dollars. Nighttime skiing was an added feature that other nearby major ski areas to Rutland—Pico and Killington—did not offer. *Courtesy Bill Jenkins.*

Above: By the mid-1960s, Birdseye was facing competition from rapidly growing and larger nearby ski areas such as Killington, Pico and Okemo. The board of directors wanted to expand Birdseye by adding a new Doppelmayr T-bar to reach higher slopes, above the north-facing Disc lift and a power line that crossed the ski area. The lift and additional trails (one being constructed is shown here) were built in 1965. None of the new trails featured snowmaking, which Jenkins deemed critical, and he resigned over the matter. A lack of natural snowfall over the following years resulted in Birdseye's closure by 1967, which might have been prevented if snowmaking was installed on the upper slopes. *Courtesy Bill Jenkins.*

Opposite top: After Birdseye closed in 1967, the land sat idle for a few years. However, in the 1970s, Don Sevigny and his father operated a campground at the base of the ski area, with campsites scattered near the now abandoned ski slopes. A large swimming pool was also installed, which can still be found as of 2010. The campground area operated for about a decade before closing in the early 1980s. In the 1980s and 1990s, Birdseye slowly returned to nature, with the slopes becoming choked with trees and the lifts rusting away. In 2003, the author and Sevigny explored Birdseye, with Sevigny pictured here standing next to the abandoned north-facing lift tower discussed previously.

Opposite bottom: Lost ski areas in Vermont tend to revert to nature rather quickly, as this view of the main slope in 2003 indicates. The slope was kept fairly clear until the early 1980s due to the campground but had mostly grown in by 2003. The Disc lift is located in the line of trees on the right, with many of the individual platters still attached to the cable. Birdseye remained quiet for a few more years but was purchased in 2006 by Ed Davis. The former ski area has been cleaned up dramatically and is now the site of the Birdseye ATV Club, which maintains the property.

GREEN MOUNTAIN COLLEGE

Above: Green Mountain College, located in Poultney, was the location of southern Vermont's only completely artificially created ski area. Bill Jenkins became Green Mountain College's ski program director in 1948 and originally taught lessons at a small rope tow area in Hampton, New York. Its distance away from campus and the short time available for lessons proved problematic. In the early 1950s, soil was excavated from nearby fields and was built into a mound of earth just behind the campus, which became the campus ski area. The ski area is shown in this campus map from the 1960s, located behind the tennis courts. *Courtesy Bill Jenkins.*

Opposite top: The ski area had a vertical drop of only 30.5 feet but was especially designed as a teaching hill. Three different gradients provided beginners, intermediates and experts the correct slope on which to practice techniques. An electric rope tow was the first lift and was just 300 feet long. Snow was often provided from city streets that was moved and bulldozed onto the slopes. The small vertical and convenience to the college proved pivotal in eliminating the fear factor of skiing; at worst, an out-of-control skier would simply glide to a stop on the flat fields surrounding the area. *Courtesy Bill Jenkins.*

Opposite bottom: Besides the main ski area, another slight drop next to it was used for beginner's lessons, shown here. More than five thousand students learned to ski at Green Mountain College in its thirty years of operation. The main hill was improved, and eventually more rope tows were added, as well as a cable disc lift that is somewhat similar to today's handle tows. An early tower-mounted snow gun, similar to a lawn sprinkler, was also installed in the 1950s and was one of Vermont's earliest snowmaking systems. *Courtesy Bill Jenkins.*

Above: Jenkins (pictured here) also instructed the Green Mountain College girls' ski team. Though not a long course by any stretch of the imagination, slalom races could be set up on the slope. With their own ski area, ski team members could practice much more than at a larger ski area. The team was quite successful, and in 1975–76, three members were named to the Division II All-East team. *Courtesy Bill Jenkins.*

Opposite bottom: Bill Jenkins utilized a skiing simulator, invented by Alois Mayer, who was the ski school director at Pico Mountain. The simulator worked by imitating the motions of turns. This also helped new skiers get a feel of what snow skiing was all about. *Courtesy Bill Jenkins.*

Jenkins frequently tried out new technologies (or invented his own) in order to enhance the skiing program at Green Mountain. Shown here is summer skiing on a soaped mat. This allowed new skiers to get a feel of what winter skiing was like prior to the snow arriving. *Courtesy Bill Jenkins.*

Another technology that allowed for out-of-season skiing was the Turfski. Turfskis were three-and-a-half-foot-long plastic skis with rollers attached at the bottom. Students could use these on any kind of slope, as long as it was lined with Uniturf (the other side of Polyturf, used in sports stadiums). Students easily made the transition from Turfskis to regular skis once the ski area opened in December. *Courtesy Bill Jenkins.*

Green Mountain College's ski area lasted until 1978, when it closed for good. The college occasionally used the hill for concerts and other events thereafter. This 2009 view of the former ski areas shows it mainly intact, with a windmill now located at its summit.

HIGH POND

High Pond Ski Area in Hubbardton was a small, secluded ski area that did offer a variety of trails and slopes. It was named after a nearby deep, clear pond that offered excellent swimming. Owner W. Douglas Burden purchased the property in the late 1940s with the intent of having a ski area for his friends. Burden was a founder and developer of Marineland of Florida and, later, Marineland of the Pacific. This sign welcomed skiers to High Pond. *Courtesy Bill Jenkins.*

In the early 1950s, access to the summit of High Pond was provided by this Bridger Platterpull lift in the background. It was a one-passenger lift that ascended a bit more than three hundred vertical feet. The rope tow pictured here was nearly flat and served a beginner's slope. *Courtesy Bill Jenkins.*

Above: Bill Jenkins and Stan Whitney managed High Pond in the early years and into the mid-1950s. They lived with their families at the nearby High Pond Inn, which they also managed. As High Pond was mostly open on weekends, Bill Jenkins was also working at this time teaching ski lessons at Green Mountain College. Jenkins remembers that, at one time, Burden's friends (who were multimillionaires) were staying at the inn for Christmas and, after the dinner was finished, shooed the Jenkinses and Whitneys out of the kitchen and did all the dishes. This view overlooks the base of the ski area and the Easy Roll slope in the distance. *Courtesy Bill Jenkins.*

Opposite top: Here cows graze on the lower slopes of High Pond in the late 1940s or early 1950s. High Pond was also a working farm, and the cows helped to keep the grass down during the summer. The Platterpull lift is visible on the right. This scene would be quite improbable at today's resorts! *Courtesy Bill Jenkins.*

Opposite bottom: While High Pond was envisioned as a mostly private ski area that did offer limited public skiing, it ended up becoming quite popular. In fact, it started to make so much money that Burden became concerned about having to pay higher taxes on the income. Eventually, the Whitneys and Jenkinses moved on to new projects later in the 1950s and left High Pond. Bill Jenkins was now teaching skiing full time at Green Mountain College in Poultney, and Stan Whitney was hired to construct Pico's base lodge. A new manager was hired, and a Doppelmayr T-bar lift was built to replace the Platterpull in the early 1960s. This 1960s view shows the scenic base area, with the T-bar lift on the left. *Courtesy Laurie Puliafico.*

High Pond's slogan ("Not one of the biggest, but one of the best!") was created by Jenkins and accurately described the ski area. This undated trail map shows the variety of skiing available. Six trails were available to all skiers. Beginners enjoyed the Just Nice and Easy Roll Trails and intermediates the Run and Hemlock, with experts choosing the Chute or the Race. Skating was also available at the pond shown here.

Right: The ski area was popular with families, who enjoyed it as an alternative to larger resorts. Caroline Curtis grew up in nearby Proctor and remembers piling into her family's Volkswagen bus and skiing nearly every weekend in the late 1960s and 1970s. Another skier, Stanzi Lucy, learned to ski here when she was three and, by age eight, had conquered all of the trails and was skiing better than her instructors! She earned an honorary patch from the ski patrol for her skiing.

Below: High Pond struggled with nearby competition, including Pico and Killington, and closed at the end of the 1977–78 ski season. It briefly reopened from 1982 to 1985 but then closed as a public ski area after 1985. However, the lift was maintained and operated privately for some time after 1985. The area remains well maintained by a caretaker. This 2008 view of the ski area shows plenty of deep snow. The lift terminal building is located in the center, with the Chute Trail still clear on the left. *Courtesy Dan Robertson.*

Although installed nearly forty years ago, the T-bar still stands, with its "Ts" still attached to the cable. The lift terminal is shown here in this 2008 photograph. Only a few trails are kept clear as of 2010, with some trails reverting back to nature. *Courtesy Dan Robertson.*

While High Pond is located on private property today, some skiers have obtained special permission to ski a few of its trails. It requires a relatively short hike up the old liftline. Here, Ryan Grace climbs the ski area to make a few runs in 2010. *Courtesy Ryan Grace.*

HYDE MANOR

Hyde Manor in Sudbury was an all-inclusive resort. The hotel was founded by Pitt Hyde in 1801, but a fire in 1862 destroyed the original structure. It was expanded in the early 1900s, and by the mid-1960s contained a bowling alley, a golf course, a farm and much more. Guests came from all over the country. In the winter, skijoring (skiing while being pulled by horses) was a popular activity. *Courtesy Ted Russell.*

In 1964, the owners built a small rope tow on their property across Route 30 on the resort golf course. John Russell was one of the builders of the tow. The tow was short, and the skiing was strictly for beginners, but it did add an extra feature to the hotel's programs during the winter. *Courtesy Ted Russell.*

Skiers would access the ski area via a short walk across Route 30. This view shows the rope tow and ski area from the hotel's porch. Skiing here was brief and lasted only four years, until 1968. Today, Hyde Manor is closed and no longer operates as a hotel; it is located on private property. *Courtesy Ted Russell.*

JENNINGS FAMILY TOW

The Jennings Family Tow was a small rope tow ski area that operated from 1963 through 1973 in Pawlet. Built by James Jennings and his father, Bill, on the Jennings Farm, the lift operated mainly for family, friends and local children. Originally four hundred feet long, it was later extended to one thousand feet. The area is located on private property today, but the lift towers, made of rot-resistant locust trees, still stand. *Courtesy James Jennings.*

RETREAT TOW

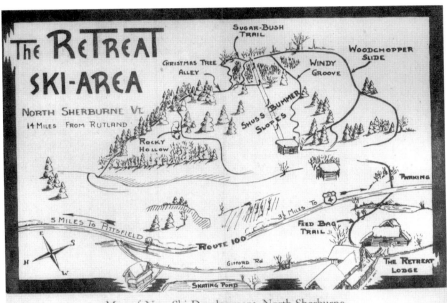

Map of New Ski Development, North Sherburne

The Retreat Ski Tow operated in North Sherburne (now Killington) from 1947 to 1950. Built and operated by Claus A. Bartenstein—a German immigrant and mechanical engineer who owned the associated Retreat Lodge—six trails were served by a six-hundred-foot rope tow. The area was a dream of Bartenstein's, who had always wanted to own his own ski area. Once the Korean War broke out in 1950, Bartenstein returned to engineering and sold the rope tow to his good friends, Brad Mead and Carl Acker, who owned Pico Ski Area. *Courtesy Anne Marie Blackman.*

SHREWSBURY SKI AREA

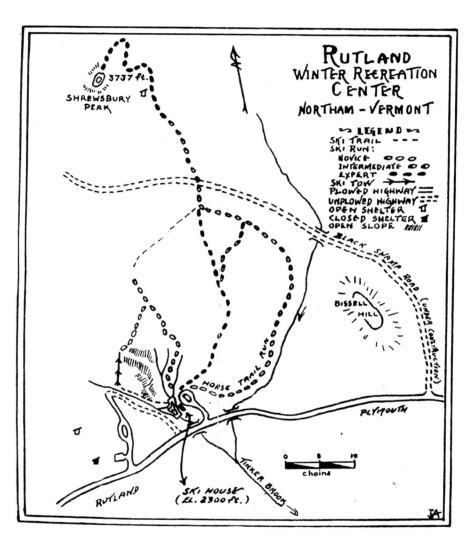

The Shrewsbury Ski Area was operated by the Rutland Ski Club and was constructed by the Civilian Conservation Corps. It was one of southern Vermont's first ski areas and was built on a road that the CCC had also constructed. Near the ski area was a "state park" called the Northam Picnic Area, which had hiking trails, campsites and the Stone House, which served as a warming hut during the winter. The tow was 1,200 feet long and opened in January, 1936. Several trails and slopes were available, including non-lift-served trails from the top of Shrewsbury Peak. Due to its high base elevation, the CCC road was hard to keep clear during the winter, and Shrewsbury Peak was closed at the beginning of World War II. *Courtesy Karen Lorentz.*

Chapter 3
LOST SKI AREAS OF
BENNINGTON COUNTY

Featuring twelve lost ski areas, Bennington County is tied with Windsor County for the least number of closed ski areas. Most of these areas were small community rope tows, such as the West Mountain Farm or the Bennington Rotary Tow. However, two of the largest lost ski areas, Snow Valley and Dutch Hill, once operated in this county. Both lasted for nearly forty years and were popular with skiers from all over New England. Both succumbed to poor snow seasons, minimal snowmaking and local competition.

The county is also home to the first overhead cable-lift ski area to close in southern Vermont, Mount Aeolus. This J-bar lift area operated in the mid-late 1930s, and its lift was later removed and installed at nearby Bromley Mountain.

The county was a popular snow train destination in the 1930s, with skiers arriving in Manchester, from which they were taken to Snow Valley or Bromley. Its proximity to New York made many of the early areas quite popular.

Today, only Bromley Ski Area remains in operation in the county.

Additional ski areas not pictured include:

Bennington Rotary, Bennington: The rotary organization operated a ski tow at the Mount Anthony Country Club in the 1960s on the ninth hole of the golf course. Later, Bennington took over the operations, but the area folded in the mid-1970s.

Bondville Tow, Bondville: This rope tow briefly operated near the bottom of what is now the Stratton Access Road in the 1940s.

Campbell Family Tow, North Bennington: This was mainly a private rope tow run by Duncan Campbell.

Horst Farm, West Bennington: Owned by Jim Horst and built by Dan Cadiz, this tow ran at the Mount Anthony Farm in the late 1950s and early 1960s.

John Clement Farm, Searsburg: Located half a mile south of Route 9 at the top of Searsburg Mountain, this rope tow briefly operated in the early 1940s. Brothers John and Lyman Clement constructed the area in February–March 1940 and offered trails for all abilities.

Leake Farm, East Bennington: Dick Leake operated this rope tow for his family on his farm from the 1940s into the early 1960s.

West Mountain Farm, Arlington: The West Mountain Farm, now the West Mountain Inn, operated a long rope tow for guests from the 1960s until 1975.

ALEX'S TOW

Alex Drysdale, an owner of a department store in Bennington, operated a ski tow at the base of Mount Prospect, about eight miles east of Bennington. The tow opened for the 1935–36 ski season and featured an 1,100-foot rope tow and skiing on several trails and slopes. One of the slopes was named the "Hedgehog," and Drysdale's tow was alternatively named the "Hedgehog Hovel Ski Area" and the "Woodford City Ski Center," depending on the year. It was closed during World War II. The area was located very close to another area, Mundell's, whose site became the much larger Mount Prospect Ski Area during the 1960s. *Courtesy Chris Lundquist.*

DUTCH HILL

The Dutch Hill Ski Area in Heartwellville was a long-lasting, compact ski area that was affectionately known as "Little Stowe" due to its challenging trail skiing. History gave it the name "Dutch Hill" due to a family of Dutch settlers who lived in the area in the 1850s. The ski area was founded in 1944 by Webster Ottman and investors from North Adams, Massachusetts, the nearest major population center. Ottman felt that there was not a lot of challenging skiing south of Stowe and that there was little skiing in the immediate area. The ski area opened for skiing in November 1944 with a one-thousand-foot-long rope tow and a few trails. *Courtesy Chris Lundquist.*

Above: At first, facilities were limited to a small warming hut and the rope tow. This continued into the following season, and in 1946, plans to expand the area commenced. New owners and North Adams businessmen David Allen, Edward Dondi and John Pedercini, along with Ottman, purchased and installed this new T-bar, as well as constructed several new trails from the summit. This increased the vertical drop to 570 feet. The first official skier of the T-bar was Adams, Massachusetts resident Adolph Konieczy, who rode the lift on its inaugural day, January 4, 1947. Originally, the lift could only carry six hundred skiers per hour to the summit, but in 1949 it was upgraded to a capacity of eight hundred skiers per hour. *Courtesy Vermont Ski Museum.*

Opposite top: Once the T-bar was installed, the original rope tow was moved to a newly purchased parcel to the north, where it was lengthened to serve the Dutch Meadows beginner's slope. This tow is shown here on the right. A new "baby" tow of three hundred feet in length was built next to the longer tow, on the left. This allowed for first-timers to use a very gentle portion of the Dutch Meadows slope. *Courtesy Vermont Ski Museum.*

Opposite bottom: Parking areas were located mostly along Route 8, with capacity for 550 cars by the late 1950s. The ski area's visibility and easy access off Route 8 made it quite popular in the 1940s through the 1960s. The Dutch Boot base lodge is visible here in the middle right. Also visible high up on the mountain slopes on the right is the Dutchman's Holiday novice trail. *Courtesy Vermont Ski Museum.*

Above: The Dutch Boot cafeteria had a capacity of one hundred and was a cozy and popular place. The large fireplace kept skiers warm, and the lodge was always packed. Also in the lodge was the Dutch Oven ski shop downstairs, along with the furnace room, which was Web Ottman's private retreat when he did not want to be found! *Courtesy Vermont Ski Museum.*

Opposite top: This 1950s trail map shows the layout of Dutch Hill. Trails fanned out along a ridge, with the steepest skiing in the middle. The Christiana and Windmill (a favorite of broadcaster Lowell Thomas) Trails were among the steepest in southern Vermont at that time. Intermediate skiers enjoyed the Yankee Doodle Trail, while beginners skied the Dyke and Dutchman's Holiday Trails and the Dutch Meadows open slope. The Dutch Meadows slope was a favorite of actress Celeste Holm, who skied there in 1955.

Opposite bottom: Most of the trails were initially narrow and rough but were graded and seeded over time, with most being able to be skied on just six to eight inches of packed snow. As the expert trails were quite difficult, they developed quite a reputation. This mogul trail is believed to be the upper portions of the Christiana Trail. It was said that if you could ski these trails at Dutch Hill, you could ski anywhere! *Courtesy Vermont Ski Museum.*

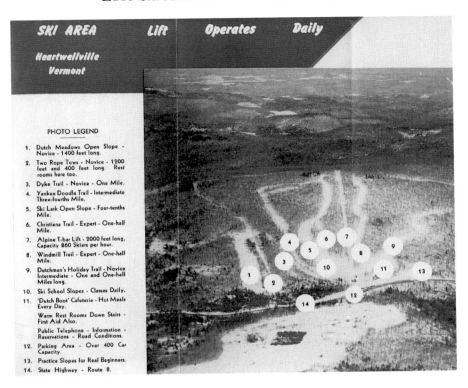

SKI AREA   Lift   Operates   Daily

Heartwellville
Vermont

PHOTO LEGEND

1. Dutch Meadows Open Slope - Novice - 1400 feet long.
2. Two Rope Tows - Novice - 1200 feet and 400 feet long. Rest rooms here too.
3. Dyke Trail - Novice - One Mile.
4. Yankee Doodle Trail - Intermediate Three-fourths Mile.
5. Ski Lark Open Slope - Four-tenths Mile.
6. Christiana Trail - Expert - One-half Mile.
7. Alpine T-bar Lift - 2000 feet long, Capacity 860 Skiers per hour.
8. Windmill Trail - Expert - One-half Mile.
9. Dutchman's Holiday Trail - Novice Intermediate - One and One-half Miles long.
10. Ski School Slopes - Classes Daily.
11. 'Dutch Boot' Cafeteria - Hot Meals Every Day.
    Warm Rest Rooms Down Stairs - First Aid Also.
    Public Telephone - Information - Reservations - Road Conditions.
12. Parking Area - Over 400 Car Capacity.
13. Practice Slopes for Real Beginners.
14. State Highway - Route 8.

One of the last major capital improvements to Dutch Hill were improvements at the base of the novice Dutch Meadows slope. In 1957, the Dutch Treat canteen (in the background) was built at the base here to provide a second cafeteria, restrooms and babysitting facilities. Later that same year, this J-bar, designed and constructed by Ottman and Dave Allen, replaced the longer rope tow that served the novice area. *Courtesy Vermont Ski Museum.*

The J-bar was a big improvement over the hard-to-ride rope tow, providing a comfortable ride to the top of the beginner's area. From here, novice skiers could ski down the Dyke Trail or use the wide-open Dutch Meadows slope. *Courtesy Vermont Ski Museum.*

Dutch Hill remained popular throughout the 1960s, but by 1968, the ski area was at its peak. The other partners were aging, and the decision was made to sell the ski area. Madelon Mulroney, who was employed at Dutch Hill as the publicity director (and considered to be one of the best in the business), is pictured here next to Web Ottman just prior to the sale of the ski area in October 1968. The two were married in 1967. After selling Dutch Hill, the Ottmans helped run the ski area for a few months with the new owners but soon retired from Dutch Hill. Madelon was also a pioneer for women in the ski industry; she also served as the secretary-treasurer of the Vermont Ski Operators Association and was a member of the New England Ski Operators Board of Directors as well. *Courtesy Vermont Ski Museum.*

Dutch Hill began to struggle in the 1970s. It was sold several times, and increasing competition from larger areas, such as Jiminy Peak and Mount Snow, began to take its toll. In 1977, the name of the ski area was changed to Dutch Mountain to try to compete with larger resorts. During the 1979–80 ski season, poor snow allowed Dutch to only open for two days and, in 1980–81, precluded it from opening altogether. Snowmaking was never installed, as the ski area usually received enough snow and water supply was limited. This 1977 view shows that the Dutch Meadows Slope was still popular for new skiers. *Courtesy John Hitchcock.*

Above: Also in the late 1960s and 1970s, a housing development called Alpenwald was started across the street. It was meant to have hundreds of chalets, but only a fraction were built. This 1977 view from this development shows the ski trails of Dutch. On the left is Dutch cross-country staff member Mike Kennedy, and on the right is Harriet Cuyler. *Courtesy John Hitchcock.*

Opposite top: Dutch did reopen in late 1981 but only operated for a few years longer. The ski area reverted back to Dutch Hill in 1981. Poor snow and high competition continued to plague the area. Manager Hank Kennedy widened the famous Christiana and Windmill Trails in 1983, as shown here in 1984. Skiers in the 1980s craved wider slopes and eschewed narrow trails, but widening the trails removed their character. Finally, after several poor seasons, Dutch Hill succumbed and was closed for good in 1985. *Courtesy John Hitchcock.*

Opposite bottom: Five years after Dutch Hill's lifts were silenced for good, the former ski area began its return back to its natural state. This March 1990 view shows the T-bar still standing between the Christiana Slope (left) and Windmill Slope (right). Both slopes had small saplings beginning to grow, which are now completely reforested as of 2010. The lift engine building and maintenance garage were still standing and in good shape. Within a decade, this view would become unrecognizable, and the buildings, including the base lodge, were burned for practice by the Readsboro Fire Department. *Courtesy John Hitchcock.*

In 1999, the area was sold to the State of Vermont and became a part of the Green Mountain Forest. All lifts and lingering man-made traces were removed, and the slopes continued to be reforested. Public access was and is allowed to the ski area, allowing anybody to explore the remains. This February 2010 view from Mattenberg Avenue across Route 8 clearly shows that the ski trails are nearly unrecognizable. *Courtesy Ryan Grace.*

Above: The formerly wide-open Dutch Meadows Slope, where many learned to ski, has grown in the least, with a few skiable lines still possible as of February 2010. The J-bar's liftline is located in the trees in the middle right. Some foundations of this lift remain visible to a hiker, and the old liftline remains fairly clear. *Courtesy Ryan Grace.*

Right: This path through the forest used to be occupied by the T-bar. It is still fairly clear, but tree growth is expanding onto the line. Aside from Dutch Meadows, the only other trail still skiable or clear enough for easy hiking is the Dutchman's Holiday novice trail, located far to the right of the ski area as one faces the hill. In a few more decades, the last lingering traces of Dutch Hill will just be a memory. *Courtesy Ryan Grace.*

MOUNT AEOLUS

Top: Mount Aeolus, located seven miles north of Manchester in East Dorset off Route 7, was one of the earliest ski areas to feature a J-bar lift. Built about 1937 by Fred Pabst, who owned Ski Tows, Inc., Aeolus's J-bar was 2,500 feet long and, for a time, was the longest aerial cable lift in the East. A huge 2,000-foot by 3,000-foot open slope and several woods trails were the main attractions. *Courtesy Vermont Ski Museum.*

Bottom: Aeolus operated into the early 1940s, and its lower elevation in a narrow valley resulted in less reliable snow cover. Fred Pabst saw the potential at nearby Bromley Mountain, uprooted the J-bar and moved it to Bromley, resulting in the closure of Mount Aeolus. Thus, Aeolus holds the record as the largest ski area to close so early in Vermont's ski history. *Courtesy Vermont Ski Museum.*

SNOW VALLEY

Right: Snow Valley, located in Winhall and very close to Bromley Mountain, began operations during the 1941–42 ski season. Snow Valley was a long-lasting ski area, open for over forty years. It faced several nearby ski resorts as competitors, including Bromley, Magic Mountain and Stratton—all of which were within a fifteen-minute or less drive away. This brochure cover is from their first season. *Courtesy Chris Lundquist.*

Below: Snow Valley was built on land that was originally owned by International Paper. In 1941, the owners, brothers Rudolph "Dolf" and Walter Rath, began clearing the ski area. Financial backing was provided by their uncle, Paul Kollsman, who had invented the altimeter used in Royal Air Force and U.S. fighter planes. Snow Valley would open with a splash: a T-bar, one of the earliest in the state. Walter was an inventor and was involved with aviation in Connecticut. The summit bullwheel of the T-bar is pictured here in later 1941, just prior to installation. *From left to right*: Walter Rath, Bunny Dillmann and architect Fritz Dillmann. *Courtesy Kathe Dillmann.*

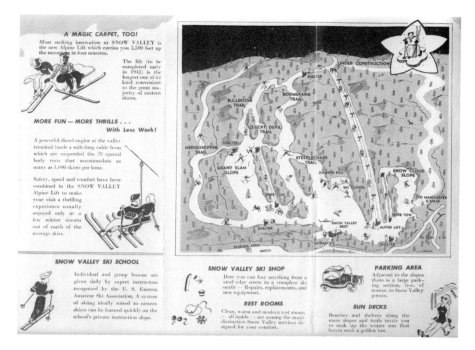

A MAGIC CARPET, TOO!

Most striking innovation at SNOW VALLEY is the new Alpine Lift which carries you 2,500 feet up the mountain in four minutes.

The lift (to be completed early in 1942) is the longest one of its kind convenient to the great majority of eastern skiers.

MORE FUN — MORE THRILLS . . .

With Less Work!

A powerful diesel engine at the valley terminal hauls a mile-long cable from which are suspended the 70 special body rests that accommodate as many as 1,000 skiers per hour.

Safety, speed and comfort have been combined in the SNOW VALLEY Alpine Lift to make your visit a thrilling experience usually enjoyed only at a few winter resorts out of reach of the average skier.

SNOW VALLEY SKI SCHOOL

Individual and group lessons are given daily by expert instructors recognized by the U. S. Eastern Amateur Ski Association. A system of skiing ideally suited to eastern skiers can be learned quickly on the school's private instruction slope.

SNOW VALLEY SKI SHOP

Here you can buy anything from a steel edge screw to a complete ski outfit — Repairs, replacements, and new equipment.

REST ROOMS

Clean, warm and modern rest rooms — all inside — are among the many distinctive Snow Valley services designed for your comfort.

PARKING AREA

Adjacent to the slopes there is a large parking section, free, of course, to Snow Valley guests.

SUN DECKS

Benches and shelters along the main slopes and trails invite you to soak up the winter sun that leaves such a golden tan.

Above: For its opening season, Snow Valley was already a major ski area. The summit T-bar—referred here in this 1941–42 trail map designed by Fritz Dillmann as an Alpine Lift—initially offered skiing on four trails at the summit that then connected with lower slopes. The ski area's signature trail, the Steeplechase, was only partially built for this year; it would later extend to the summit. Beginners had their choice of two rope tows, with easy skiing off the Grand Slam and Snow Cloud Slope. Route 30 used to pass directly at the bottom of the ski area, providing direct access from Manchester; however, the road was steep, icy and treacherous in the winter and was later rerouted. A new entrance to Snow Valley was created several years later. *Courtesy Chris Lundquist.*

Opposite top: Fritz Dillmann, pictured here, designed Snow Valley's base lodge, the Snow Man's Rest. Ernst Durban was also an associate in its design. This lodge was featured in *Architectural Forum* as "breaking away from traditional log cabin style, establishes a pleasant background pattern for America's latest popular sport." In a 1940s brochure, the lodge was described as a "welcome haven for the weary…a club in the clouds with an observation deck and a sun deck…strains of lilting music floating through the air…a vast fireplace and wholesome Vermont food, piping hot, to the king's taste." *Courtesy Kathe Dillmann.*

Opposite bottom: The view of base area is seen in this 1950s postcard. From left to right are the T-bar and rope tow base terminals, the Snow Man's Rest and the waxing room and ski shop. A parking lot was found behind the lodge. A steep incline from the base lodge to the access road made it quite difficult for cars to exit if the road was icy. In its first years of operation, some skiers were brought to the mountain via horse and wagon after arriving on ski trains in Manchester.

Top: The Steeplechase Slope was Snow Valley's signature trail. It was wide and moderately steep and was the most visible from Snow Man's Rest. A large boulder in the middle of the trail was often used as a jump. The T-bar liftline is on the left, paralleling the Steeplechase Slope through the woods. Buzz Eichel remembers that in the 1950s the T-bar operated with a turnstile, with the cost of each lift ride being twenty-five cents!

Bottom: Snow Valley featured a ski school that was recognized as one of the most outstanding ski schools in the East. A brochure described it as "being staffed by competent Certified Ski Instructors, noted for their special success with all types of skier's problems, from beginner to expert. Also under their supervision and guidance is the Ski Patrol which services the entire area and makes skiing safe for everyone." Here, a lesson gathers outside the Snow Man's Rest.

The Worthy Inn in Manchester (later the Village Country Inn) was a popular place for Snow Valley skiers to stay, and in fact it was owned by Snow Valley in the later 1940s. The inn provided transportation to Snow Valley, which was about ten to fifteen minutes away. The ski area was later sold to Fred and Mary Colclough, who also purchased the Worthy Inn.

Fritz Dillmann designed many of the ski area's original pieces of artwork in the 1940s, including this original poster. By the 1960s, the ski area was sold again, this time to Mr. Ladd Parker and his wife, Avis. The area became more known as a local mountain, catering toward budget-friendly skiers. It remained a popular local ski area during this time and was known for its parties, races and good fun. Nearby areas such as Bromley, Stratton and Magic Mountain were expanding during this time, and the Parkers developed plans to add a summit chairlift; however, this would not come to fruition until 1976 under different owners. *Courtesy Kathe Dillmann.*

77

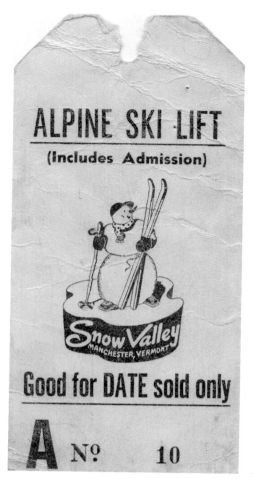

Left: After the Parkers owned the ski area, it was sold again, this time to John Frohling, about 1970. He owned the ski area until it closed in 1984. Clark Comollo was a manager here in the early 1970s and remembers that all employees pitched in, including himself, for clearing trails in the summer, selling tickets, doing lift maintenance and more. Later in the 1970s, Rick Birmingham became a part-time marketing director and worked with manager Doug Wilk to improve the grooming, install some basic snowmaking equipment and add a cafeteria and arcade, to make the area as competitive as it could be.

Below: In 1976, Snow Valley expanded its lift capacity with a brand-new Borvig Double Chairlift. It was situated lower than the T-bar (which was shortly removed) and expanded the vertical of the area to 630 feet. This early 1980s trail map shows the final layout of the mountain. The St. Christopher Trail had been named after Ladd Parker's son, Chris, and the Peter Pan Slope was named after Peter Colclough, Fred and Mary Colclough's son. *Courtesy New England Ski Museum*

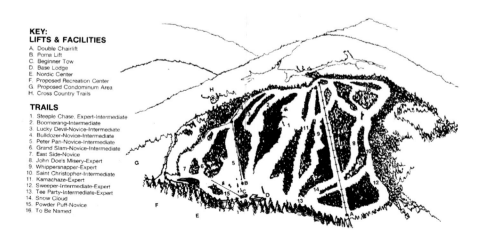

KEY:

LIFTS & FACILITIES

A. Double Chairlift
B. Poma Lift
C. Beginner Tow
D. Base Lodge
E. Nordic Center
F. Proposed Recreation Center
G. Proposed Condominum Area
H. Cross Country Trails

TRAILS

1. Steeple Chase. Expert-Intermediate
2. Boomerang-Intermediate
3. Lucky Devil-Novice-Intermediate
4. Bulldozer-Novice-Intermediate
5. Peter Pan-Novice-Intermediate
6. Grand Slam-Novice-Intermediate
7. East Side-Novice
8. John Doe's Misery-Expert
9. Whippersnapper-Expert
10. Saint Christopher-Intermediate
11. Kamachaze-Expert
12. Sweeper-Intermediate-Expert
13. Tee Party-Intermediate-Expert
14. Snow Cloud
15. Powder Puff-Novice
16. To Be Named

Snow Valley has an important distinction of being one of the first ski areas to fully embrace snowboarding. In fact, in 1983 and 1984, Snow Valley hosted the National Snowboarding Championship (now the Burton U.S. Open). In the early 1980s, Snow Valley also heavily advertised to local colleges, including offering bunk-style accommodations for just ten dollars per night, movies, barbecues, full racing facilities, snowboarding competitions, a Winter Carnival and more. However, despite the valiant attempts at keeping Snow Valley operational, it folded in 1984. This later postcard shows the final aerial view of the ski slopes near the end of Snow Valley's operation.

Above: After closing, Snow Valley was heavily vandalized, but the lifts remained on the property and the lodges remained standing. The slopes became heavily forested. In 2004, the land was purchased by Chris Franco and his family, who plan to eventually redevelop the property into a private ski area with homes. In 2005, NELSAP enthusiasts were granted permission to ski the recently cleared trails and slopes at Snow Valley. It was a strictly "earn your turns" affair. With two feet of fresh powder, bluebird skies and fantastic views, the experience of enjoying this lost ski area was one not to be forgotten. Here, skiers climb the Steeplechase Slope with a view of Bromley Mountain in the background.

Opposite top: Snow Valley remains clearly visible from the summit of nearby Bromley Mountain. Most prominent is the steep and wide Steeplechase Slope, which is central in this 2008 photograph. At the far right, one can just make out the twisting intermediate trail, St. Christopher. *Courtesy Duncan McNeill.*

Opposite bottom: In the late 1970s, the base lodge was expanded to include a second floor and more seating area, as well as a deck to overlook the slopes. Once abandoned in the early to mid-1980s, the lodge was vandalized and stripped to the walls, though the large central fireplace remained intact. As of 2010, this former base lodge remains in a state of disrepair and cannot be salvaged. *Courtesy Dan Robertson.*

The 1976 Borvig Double Chairlift remains standing in this 2008 photograph, though one can clearly see that nature is taking over. For the most part, the old liftline has returned to forest. Chairs that last served skiers nearly thirty years ago still dangle from the lift, surrounded by trees. While not pictured here, the Pomalift also remains standing. *Courtesy Dan Roberston.*

WINHALL SNOW BOWL

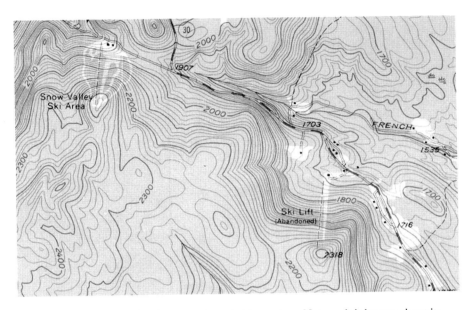

The Winhall Snow Bowl is a lost area shrouded in mystery. Not much is known about its brief operation. It is believed that the area was constructed and operated only for a few years in the early 1950s, with a homemade wooden J-bar style of lift and one wide, open slope. This 1957 topographic map shows the location of the Snow Bowl, with its then already-abandoned lift, just a few miles from Snow Valley. *Courtesy University of New Hampshire Library Digital Collections Initiative.*

Left: Winhall Snow Bowl was clearly visible from the summit of Bromley Mountain, three miles away, as this 1950s photograph shows. One can make out the one wide-open slope on the left and liftline on the right. It is believed that an attempt to reopen the area occurred in the early 1970s but failed. *Courtesy Don Cosgrove.*

Below: Today, the area is private property and has nearly completely returned to its natural state. However, some remnants of the lift remain, including this portion of the engine. Much of the slope and liftline have grown in, though parts of the liftline are still visible. *Courtesy Joe Morein.*

Chapter 4
LOST SKI AREAS OF WINDHAM COUNTY

Windham County holds the distinction for having the highest number of lost ski areas in southern Vermont, at nineteen. Brattleboro was an initial hot spot for skiing, with several rope tow ski areas located in town no longer in operation. This was a popular snow train destination, as well.

The county was also home to a few major ski areas that have been lost. Family-operated Hogback was a very popular ski area that operated for forty years, from the mid-1940s until the mid-1980s. High insurance costs sank the ski area, just as they have done to many other areas in southern Vermont. Maple Valley was the other large ski area that has been lost in the county, and although the lifts and lodge are intact, it is unlikely to reopen in the future.

At the time of this writing in 2010, Haystack Ski Area/Haystack Club in Wilmington was in flux. It has been closed for the past several years, but there are plans to reopen the area as a private club with limited access for town residents. In December 2009, the ski area operated for town residents and prospective home buyers for a few days, but this did not continue for the rest of the season. Disagreements over water rights with Mount Snow continue. As it is inconclusive whether Haystack Club will fully reopen, it is being left off the "lost" list for now.

Mount Snow, Stratton Mountain and Magic Mountain are the remaining large resorts that continue to operate in the county. Two smaller community areas, Rockingham Recreation and Living Memorial Park, are the last remnants of small ski areas in southern Vermont, and more information on them can be found in the "Survivors" chapter.

Additional ski areas not pictured include:

Big Prospect, Dummerston: Terry Tyler built the rope tow here, which was owned by Dr. David Baldwin on the East-West Road. It began operations in 1953 but was closed by 1962 and was never profitable.

Bonnyvale Tow, West Brattleboro: Operating on Bonnyvale Road, this rope tow area was in existence in the 1940s. Paul Robinson, who skied here as a child in the 1940s, remembers narrow trails at the top that broadened out into a large meadow.

Doctor Otis Tow, Townshend: According to Bob Weir, Dr. Otis ran a rope tow behind his house that was used mainly by local children.

Glendale Ski Area, Newfane: Raymond "Pete" Severance operated this ski area on land owned by the Sadler family on South Wardsboro Road. It was open from the mid-1950s to the early 1960s. Skiers going too fast at the bottom would often end up in Smith Brook!

Little Prospect, Dummerston: Also built by Terry Tyler, this area was owned by Randy Hickins on the East-West Road. A rope tow operated from 1952 to 1957. A small snack bar was also available.

New England Kurn Hattin Home, Westminster: Kurn Hattin Home provided services for children and families and briefly ran a short rope tow in the late 1960s and early 1970s.

North River Ski Area, Halifax: Joseph Darrow operated a five-hundred-foot-long rope tow in the late 1940s and early 1950s, and it was mainly used for weekends, holidays and special parties.

Tater Lane Tow, Brattleboro: This rope tow briefly operated in the 1940s on Tater Lane, now known as South Street.

Vermont Academy Tow, Saxton's River: Started by Coach Warren Chivers, this area was used mostly by students during the week and locals on the weekend. Bob Cambell, who was a student, states that the most memorable part of the ski area was its incredibly fast rope tow. It operated from the 1950s until 1997, and the tow was dismantled in 2002.

Wilmington Tow, Wilmington: A one-thousand-foot rope tow operated in the village in the late 1930s and the 1940s.

Windham College, Putney: Open from the 1960s until 1975, the college had a short rope tow for students. Rob Muller, who was a student here, remembers the area being called "Freak Peak" due to the high amount of hippie students!

BURRINGTON HILL

Burrington Hill in Whitingham was a classic family-owned ski area. Owned and operated by Chet and Darthy Page, the ski area began operating in the late 1950s and featured five trails on a 150-foot vertical drop. A high base elevation for a small ski area (nearly 1,900 feet) helped maintain snow longer than lower elevations.

NEW, MODERN CABLE LIFT

ROPE TOW ON BEGINNERS SLOPE

SKATING & TOBOGGANING

SNACK BARN

SKI SHOP & RENTALS

COZY ATMOSPHERE,

EXCELLENT FOOD

IDEAL FOR FAMILIES

SKI INSTRUCTIONS

BURRINGTON HILL & SKI LODGE
in the ♥ of So. Vermont Ski Area

RATES
Lift $2.50 Weekdays - $3.00 Sat. Sun. Holidays
Jr. Lift 1.50 "   2.00   "
Rope tow 1.00 "   1.00   "

Phone: JACKSONVILLE EMpire 8-2309

Darthy and Chet Page

Like most southern Vermont family areas, additional activities beyond skiing were provided. Many visitors enjoyed skating and tobogganing and were even offered a heated outdoor swimming pool later in the 1960s. A small snack barn and a ski shop with rentals were available. Rates were very affordable—in this 1960s brochure, tickets were only $2.50 for weekdays and $3.00 for weekends. Limited lodging was available at the farmhouse.

Bill Jenkins, who operated Birdseye Mountain in Castleton, built Burrington Hill's Disc lift in the late 1950s. This was a very unique lift and was one of only three ever made (the other two were at Green Mountain College in Poultney and at Temple Mountain in New Hampshire). Unlike most platter-type lifts, this one was connected to the lift cable at a ninety-degree angle. In this 1959 view, skiers ride up the disc lift. *Courtesy Bill Jenkins.*

In order to prevent damage to the lift carriers, the discs were removed after the ski season in the spring. The smooth liftline, with the discs removed for the summer, is visible in this May 1964 photo. For advertising, Burrington Hill called itself "The Smallest Ski Area in the World" as a nod to Mount Snow, which billed itself as the largest. *Courtesy Bill Jenkins.*

Chet Page, seen here at the top of the disc lift, operated the ski area until the early 1970s. Carl Yettru, who skied here in the late 1960s, remembers the friendliness and hospitality of the Pages. His sons particularly enjoyed the heated outdoor pool, and he recalls that he and his wife had a hard time getting them to leave. On one trip on the morning of departure, a huge snowstorm provided amazing ski conditions, and the Pages were concerned for the Yettrus, as they had to return to New York. They offered another night of lodging, but the Yettrus had to leave—even though they were very tempted to stay! Burrington Hill closed in 1971 and reopened in 1974 when Ed Tanny purchased the area, but tough economic times and high energy prices closed the ski area in 1978. The area is private property today. *Courtesy Bill Jenkins.*

HOGBACK

Hogback Mountain Ski Area (built on Mount Olga) was located at the height of land between Wilmington and Brattleboro on Route 9. It opened on land owned by Harold White for the 1946–47 ski season and was operated by Hogback Mountain Ski Lift Company, a corporation based in Brattleboro. John Dunham was the president of the corporation. For its inaugural season, Hogback featured a Constam T-bar, which could serve nine hundred skiers per hour, the highest capacity lift in the United States at that time. *Courtesy Brian Wyckoff.*

Ripperoo was a wide, cascading intermediate slope that was quite popular and was accessed from the top of the T-bar. It was also the slope used for the weekend Hogback Standard Races, which began during the 1949–50 ski season. To the skier's right of this trail were the Glade and Meadow novice runs, where beginners could progress after mastering the Practice Slope.

Marlboro Inn—food and lodging, wonderful views.

"It really Snows at Hogback . . ." Good food here, too.

Hogback had a unique layout, as depicted here in this early 1950s trail map. Skiers would begin their day at Route 9, where they could find food available at the Skyline Restaurant operated by Dick and Joyce Hamilton. From there, beginners could ride a rope tow on the Practice Slope, where the novice Tower Trail was available as well. Intermediate and expert skiers would ski down Rim Run or the Basin Trails to reach the main T-bar. Additional trails and slopes were available from the top of this lift. Lodging was available at the Marlboro Inn located near the ski area. The inn was operated by Harold White's son, Arnold, and his wife, Ruth, from 1951 to 1957. The family lived at the inn with their two daughters, Sally and Suzanne, during this time. Arnold spent his entire working career at Hogback.

Above: The trails at Hogback served by the Constam T-bar were quite scenic, often lined with spruce trees caked in snow. Hogback ranged in elevation from approximately 1,900 feet to 2,400 feet. This high elevation helped preserve the natural snow longer than lower elevation areas. Hogback was located in what is called the "120 Inch Snow Belt," a high annual snowfall area along Green Mountains. In the background, one can also see Mount Snow.

Opposite top: "Bottom Warmer" was the name affectionately given to this Quonset hut located at the base of the main T-bar. Hotdogs, hamburgers, snacks and hot coffee were often on the menu. A serving window allowed skiers to order and get their food from outside, or they could eat indoors in a small dining area. Food needed to be brought down via sled, as there were no roads leading to the Bottom Warmer. Dick Hamilton, who managed the food services at Hogback, remembers one time when he was bringing donuts to the hut, which spilled out accidentally into the snow; Hamilton joked that he now had had "frosted" donuts available! Later, the hut was expanded with a new kitchen.

Opposite bottom: Hogback Mountain's ski patrol took pride in their work keeping skiers safe. The photo shows the patrol assisting a fallen skier on the Practice Slope. The ski patrol was all-volunteer. At the summit of the main T-bar was "The Castle," the patrol's headquarters on the mountain from which they could access the entire area. *Photo by Lewis Brown, Courtesy the Marlboro Historical Society*.

Hogback was an excellent ski area to learn the sport and featured a top-notch ski school. In the late 1940s and early 1950s, the school was operated by the High Mountain Ski School of New York City, directed by Joe Ritter. Tino Koch, a multilingual head of the ski school, came from Switzerland, where he had nearly thirty years of ski teaching experience. Here, skiers make their way to the Practice Slope in the 1950s. The original ski shop is visible in the background, and further back is the Skyline Restaurant. The original ski shop was a small building that featured retail on one side, rentals on the other and a potbellied stove in the middle. According to Ruth White, a sign hung over the wood stove warning skiers not to get too close—skiers occasionally did, and many found the backs of their nylon parkas completely melted.

Jim Howard ran the ski school for much of the 1950s and 1960s. He was a veteran United States Eastern Amateur Ski Association (USEASA) certified instructor, as well as a professional ski instructor of America. In the mid-1950s and into the early 1960s, Cliff Taylor, a ski instructor, developed what he called "Shortee Skis," where one would learn skiing on very short skis. The short skis allowed for quick turning and could have new skiers learning parallel turns within a day. They would often utilize the Practice Slope, shown here in the 1950s. *Courtesy Don Cosgrove.*

In 1955, a new Pomalift was constructed on the northeast slopes of the ski area. This lift was created to increase the visibility of the ski area, as drivers on Route 9 could now easily see one of Hogback's lift. The original T-bar was not visible from Route 9. This image shows the construction of one of the lower towers of the lift at the end of 1955. Additional trails were created near the Poma to increase ski terrain. *Photo by Lewis Brown, Courtesy the Marlboro Historical Society.*

Sylvia Lundsted Johnson is pictured here as she loads the new Pomalift. Johnson was a waitress who worked at the Skyline Restaurant at Hogback. Employee Chet Long assists her as she loads the high speed, detachable lift. Pomas detached from the main cable, once loaded, to provide a quick trip to the top. *Photo by Lewis Brown. Courtesy the Marlboro Historical Society.*

One of the new trails created by the Pomalift was the Molly Stark Trail, a seventy-five-foot-wide intermediate trail. The clearing of the trail is shown here in this image, likely taken prior to the 1955–56 ski season. For the 1956–57 season, the Molly Stark and the Great White Way (a two-hundred-foot-wide slope also served by the Pomalift) were smoothed and seeded with grass so that they could be skied on a minimum of six inches of snow. *Photo by Lewis Brown. Courtesy the Marlboro Historical Society.*

This aerial view of the Pomalift-served section of the ski area shows the wide Great White Way slope as the main feature of the area. A rope tow also ran for a time along the left side of the slope, which can be made out here. The Pomalift ran up the narrow liftline to the right of the Great White Way, and to the right of the lift was the Molly Stark. Later, another trail—the narrow Intermediate Olga—was built to the right of the Molly Stark.

The Alpenglo Restaurant and Lodge was constructed in 1960 at the base of the Practice Slope in order to provide for more skier services. Located along Route 9, it featured a restaurant/snack bar, operated by Dick and Joyce Hamilton, on the top floor. On the lower floor were the Hogback Ski School and the Hogback Ski and Gift Shop, operated by Arnold White and co-managed by Brandon Douglas. The Ski and Gift Shop sold sundries and ski clothing and was also a place where Douglas repaired damaged ski equipment. The lower floor also featured a day lodge space, as well as a place to eat boxed lunches. Also on the Hogback property, next to the Marlboro Inn, was the Hogback Gift Shop, which featured the Luman Nelson Museum. According to Sally White, families would ski all day in the winter and then bring their children afterward to the museum, which was installed by Harold White, to learn about local species of birds and animals.

Hogback remained a popular family ski area in the 1960s, and due to this growth, two more new Doppelmayr T-bar lifts were installed in 1964. One was built to parallel the original T-bar lift (pictured here) and was named the Meadow T-bar. The Constam T-bar became known as the Sugar T-bar and was replaced by another new lift in 1971 after a fire destroyed the engine room. The other 1964 T-bar was installed along the skier's left side of the Practice Slope, running into the woods near the summit, and was the named the Alpenglo lift. This new beginner's lift allowed for easier access to easy terrain as compared to the original rope tow.

HOGBACK SKI AREA

1. Glade – Novice
2. Meadow – Novice
3. Ripperoo – Intermediate
4. Razorback – Expert
5. Twin T-Bar Lift #2
6. Twin T-Bar Lift #1
7. Sugar Slope – Intermediate
8. Cutoff – Intermediate
9. Squeal – Intermediate
10. Basin – Expert
11. Rim Run – Intermediate
12. Practice Slope – Novice
13. "Alpenglo" T-Bar Lift #3
14. Tower – Novice
15. Rope Tow
16. Great White Way – Novice
17. "Whiteway" #4 T-Bar Lift
18. Molly Stark – Intermediate
19. Olga – Intermediate
20. Alpenglo Lodge
21. Warming Hut
22. Warming Hut
23. Gift Shop
24. Skyline Restaurant
25. Marlboro Inn

TWO AREAS IN ONE

Hogback offers two complete areas—one featuring a high capacity T-Bar Lift and a Rope Tow on the north side of the mountain and three other T-Bars on the east and southeast. The top terminals of each of the lifts are close together at the top of the mountain, meaning skiers have easy access to all 14 of Hogback's trails and slopes which have been smoothed and grassed so as to be skiable on the minimum of snow cover. Except on a few extremely busy weekends this should eliminate any long waiting lines, meaning more time for skiing and less time waiting, one of the reasons you will want to ski Hogback again and again.

Ski More... Discover HOGBACK

Hogback reached its peak size in the early 1970s, as shown here in this trail map. In 1969, the Pomalift was removed, and a new T-bar was installed to take its place. A few years later, the rope tow on the Great White Way was removed. In the mid-1970s, Harold White's children and families—including Arnold and Ruth White, Brandon and Betsy (White) Douglas and Dick and Joyce (White) Hamilton—bought the ski area. Hogback was now truly a family-owned ski area. At that time, Arnold and Ruth White were operating the gift and rental shop, the Marlboro Inn, the museum and other rental properties; the Douglases were involved with Ski Shop; and the Hamiltons were involved with the Skyline Restaurant and the Alpenglo. Other full-time employees at the ski area were Mountain Manager Russell Southworth, as well as Holland Douglas, Brandon Douglas's brother. Hogback continued to be a family ski area, with season tickets for children as low as twenty-five dollars during this time. *Courtesy Chris Lundquist.*

The ski area was very popular with kids, especially for jumping. The ski school started making jumps using hay bales every once in a while. Pictured here is Brian Wyckoff jumping off a jump in 1974 as a fourteen-year-old. To the right, looking at the jump, is Bill Douglas, head of the ski school at that time. The concept of terrain parks that are heavily used as ski areas is certainly nothing new. *Courtesy Brian Wyckoff.*

By the early 1980s, insurance rates and a few poor snow seasons began to take their toll on Hogback. By Hogback's last season of 1985–86, insurance rates exceed the area's entire gross income, and Hogback had to be shut down. The Whites continued to operate the gift shop and the Hamiltons, the Skyline restaurant, until 1993; then the property was auctioned off. Trails began to grow in with vegetation, and the ski area slowly began to return to nature. Future skiers would no longer be able to learn to ski or enjoy the lift-served slopes at Hogback. Photo of the Practice Slope and T-bar, 1970s. *Courtesy Brian Wyckoff.*

Despite being closed, the gift shops and the museum remained open and operated by Arnold White until the properties were sold in 1993. The area surrounding Hogback was and continues to be popular. Tourists still enjoy the one-hundred-mile view from Route 9, and the Southern Vermont Natural History Museum (www.vermontmuseum.org), founded in 1996 next to the Scenic View, provides an excellent experience to learn about Vermont's natural environment and features Luman Nelson's collection. In this 2007 image, all that remains of the original beginner's rope tow at Hogback is this partially grown-in liftline and one pulley mounted on the tree. One can see the Practice Slope to the right of the liftline, through the woods.

The Bottom Warmer hut at the bottom of the Twin T-bars has seen better days but remains standing. Part of the outer wall has collapsed. Inside the building were kitchen equipment nearly intact, picnic tables and restrooms, left just the way they were when the last skiers used them in 1985. Sadly, the building is no longer "sunbathing headquarters on spring days," as was it referred to in a 1950s brochure.

The Twin T-bars that hauled countless skiers to the summit remain standing in this 2007 image. While still clear enough for hiking, the old liftline is becoming choked with new tree growth. Fencing that once served as a corral for liftlines has partially collapsed.

One of the trails served by the two T-bars was the expert Razorback. A steep, narrow and twisting trail, Razorback was the most difficult at Hogback. In 2007, it remained nearly clear enough to ski, save for a few fallen trees.

The last tower near the summit of Twin T-bar #1 remains standing, though the liftline is entangled with plant growth. On the left is the former ski patrol summit building, "The Castle," which also remains standing and in fairly good shape considering the more than twenty years since the area last operated.

Rare at Vermont and New England ski areas was this bridge, which carried skiers riding the Practice/Alpenglo #3 Lift over the novice Tower Trail. This ski bridge was no longer safe to walk across in 2007, but it was still standing.

This T-bar, the Whiteway #4 Lift, which had replaced the Pomalift, remains nearly intact (though rusty), minus the Ts themselves. The liftline was clear, as were the neighboring trails, Molly Stark and Olga.

There has been interest in preserving Hogback's land from development since its closure in 1986. In 2005, the Marlboro Conservation Commission held a public meeting to see if there was interest in preserving the mountain, and in April 2006, fifteen volunteers formed the Hogback Mountain Conservation Association (HMCA) to look into preserving the land, which was for sale. Two years later, a private group was able to purchase the property from Skyline Partners in order to preserve the property. Much planning and fundraising was done by the HMCA and the Vermont Land Trust to save Hogback, and by March 2010, the goals were met, those involved with the land purchase were paid back and the property was sold to the Town of Marlboro. The former ski area is now open to the public for passive recreation, including backcountry and cross-country skiing, hiking and nature study. For more information, visit www.hogback.org. This February 2010 view shows that the Practice Slope is still recognizable and easily explored from Route 9.

LATCHIS PARK

Latchis Ski Park was a relatively brief rope tow ski area that operated in Brattleboro from the late 1940s into the 1950s. Owned and operated by John Latchis and the Latchis Hotel, the ski park boasted having ten thousand watts of lighting for nighttime skiing, a 1,200-foot rope tow, a thirty-five-meter expert training jump and a ten-meter ski jump. The smaller jump was developed by owner John Latchis and Fred Harris, a veteran jumper. The construction of an exit ramp for Route 91 isolated the area, resulting in its closure.

MAPLE VALLEY

ROUTE 30
WEST DUMMERSTON, VERMONT 05357

SKI
Maple Valley

Ski
Maple
Valley

Valley Shop
Restaurant
Ski shop   Cafeteria   Lounge
(802) 254-6083

Maple Valley Ski Area in West Dummerston was a classic family ski area that operated from 1963 through 1999, though it was closed for a few years during that time. The ski area was built and owned by Angelo, Joe and Frank Pirovane. Angelo was the president and co-owner of North Haven Construction Company, along with his two brothers. Angelo had also built and was a co-owner of Enchanted Mountain Ski Area in Maine. Terry Tyler was the first manager of the ski area and was also involved with its construction.

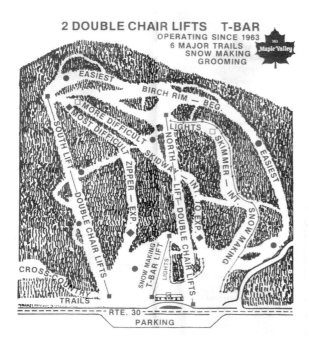

2 DOUBLE CHAIR LIFTS   T-BAR
OPERATING SINCE 1963
6 MAJOR TRAILS
SNOW MAKING
GROOMING

Maple Valley

SEASON PASSES	
Adults $150.00	
18 YRS. OR IN SCHOOL	
Juniors $100.00	

FAMILY PASSES	
Father	$150.00
Mother	135.00
First Child	100.00
Second Child	75.00
Third Child	75.00
Fourth or more	50.00
Under Six	Free

LIFT TICKET RATES

Saturday,	Sunday,	Holidays,
		Half-day (1 PM)
Adults $15.00		Adults $12.00
Juniors $13.00		Juniors $10.00

Weekdays (non-holiday)

		Half-day (1 PM)
Adults $10.00		Adults $6.00
Juniors $7.50		Juniors $5.00

SKI SHOP RENTALS

Equipment	Full Day	Half Day (1 PM)
Skis, boots, poles	$12.00	$10.00
Skis, boots	$10.00	$8.00
Skis, poles	$8.00	$7.00
Skis	$7.00	$6.00
Boots	$7.00	$6.00
Poles	$2.00	$2.00

Above: During its first year of operation, Maple Valley offered skiing on a T-bar and a summit South Double Chair, both Hall-brand lifts, as well as a beginner's rope tow. The vertical drop was 820 feet. The following year, in 1964, another double chairlift was added to assist with the crowds. Initially, trails were referred to as Trails 1–5, though they did have official names, as shown here in this early 1980s trail map. A twisty beginner's trail underneath the South Double Chair was called the "Squeezer," as it was quite narrow. A ski jump was available at the top of the T-bar slope for a few years before it was removed.

Opposite bottom: The base lodge was also opened during the summer as a gift shop, featuring Vermont products, as well as a restaurant. In the wintertime, music was projected from the base lodge into the lower portions of the ski area. Once, Charley Purinton asked his son, Chris, to go to Brattleboro to buy popular music—and according to Nick, the same songs were played over and over again for years! By the late 1970s and the early 1980s, Maple Valley struggled against local competition, as it was located on Route 30, the gateway to larger areas such as Stratton and Bromley. A lack of snowmaking also hurt the area during lean years.

Charley Purinton became the president of the ski area in 1966 until the late 1970s. This period of time, particularly in the late 1960s and early 1970s, was Maple Valley's most popular. Charley's son, Nick, remembers how many of the skiers were regulars and season pass holders from the Springfield/Longmeadow, Massachusetts and Hartford, Connecticut area. Maple Valley had a strong local program with schools, and many nearby kids learned to ski here. Nick also remembers that the T-bar had nighttime skiing and that sometimes, as the area was so popular, the lines for all the lifts would merge into one mass. The liftline is shown here on the summit chair in the 1960s. *Courtesy Chris Lundquist.*

Left: Financial troubles resulted in the ski area not opening during the 1988–89 ski season, but it did reopen the following season. Upgrades to the mountain were made—with some additional snowmaking and nighttime skiing from the summit—but the area remained dependent on natural snow. A snowboard halfpipe was added in the early 1990s. However, the area had a good "vibe" to it—as the author can attest to, skiing here with his family in 1994. The trails were fun, everybody was having a good time and it was a truly enjoyable ski area. This 1990s brochure refers to the skiing here as "The way skiing should be, the way it used to be!"—which was very true.

Below: More troubles ensued, and the ski area did not open for the 1996–97 or 1997–98 ski seasons. A new owner during that time had considered using trucks to ferry skiers to the summit, but this did not occur. The area reopened, though, for the 1999–2000 season briefly but then closed for good. Pictured here is the T-bar in February 2005. *Courtesy Dan Robertson.*

Above: Maple Valley's "South" Double Chair that reached the summit is still intact, as shown here in this 2007 photo. The length of lift was exaggerated in this sign; it was really three thousand feet long. Trees and brush continue to encroach upon the lift as of 2010. *Courtesy Dan Robertson.*

Right: The North Double chair also remains at Maple Valley in this 2007 view. The slope below, later called the Sugar Bowl, remained mostly open, with only a few saplings on the slope. The base lodge remains in good shape, as does the T-bar. *Courtesy Dan Robertson.*

PINE TOP

The Pine Top Ski area operated from the late 1940s to about 1960 on Pelley Hill in South Vernon. It was located on the grounds of a lodge named Stonehurst. Operated by Romy and Elsie Racine, Pine Top featured a complete experience, with affordable lodging available at the ski area. In this 1953 advertisement, a package of skiing and two meals were just seven dollars per day!

Pine Top ski area featured two rope tows, including the one pictured here. Nighttime skiing was also available here, which was rare at many ski areas. In the 1950s, there were often heated discussions between ski areas about whether to offer nighttime skiing or not. Arguments against included the cold, skiers being tired from working all day and poor lighting. Arguments for included more time for skiers during the week, as well as time for more instruction and practice. Ultimately though, the arguments against won out, and today most Vermont ski areas do not offer nighttime skiing. *Courtesy Tim Ingalls.*

The operators of Pine Top and another Windham County area, Sugar Bush, were friends and would sometimes direct skiers to the other ski area if skiing was not available at their location. Pine Top operated until 1960. Pictured here is Robert Earle with his daughter, Nancy, at the top of the rope tow, with Brenda Patnode behind them. *Courtesy Nancy Leavy.*

THE PUTNEY SCHOOL

The Putney School operated a rope tow that was used primarily for students, beginning in the mid-1930s. During the 1940s and 1950s, students were required to learn how to ski. According to Harriet Rogers, the more experienced students taught the less experienced ones to ski, and they would become experienced enough to visit a larger mountain by the end of the season. This ski jump was also available for students. *Courtesy The Putney School.*

Countless students learned to ski here, and the rope tow operated until 1976. It was then closed until 1981, where it remained open until 1990. Matt Syrett, class of 1985, remembered that the speedy rope tow was "powered by a surplus tank engine, which would almost pull your arm out of your socket." The lift finally gave out, and the ski area was closed in 1990. This 1950s view from the top of the ski area shows the surrounding countryside, with the rope tow at the lower left. *Courtesy The Putney School.*

SKI BOWL, INC.

Right: Ski Bowl, Inc., located in Saxton's River, was constructed by Robert Hogarth Sr. on his property in 1936. It opened for skiers in 1937 and was run by the Hogarths through 1941. According to his son, Bill, Hogarth developed the ski area not due to a deep passion for the sport but rather to supplement the farm's income during the winter months. This was common with many early ski areas. Featuring a ski hut, a one-thousand-foot-long rope tow, four trails, a beginner's slope and a wide-open ski bowl, Ski Bowl, Inc., was a substantial ski area. Bob Hogarth Jr. remembers that the Hurricane of 1938 blew many trees down on the property, which he helped clear. *Courtesy Ellen Howard.*

Below: Unique to the Ski Bowl was the fact that skiers did not drive and park directly at the ski area. Rather, they parked at an area just off Route 121, from which a shuttle bus would carry them to the ski area. Here, skiers load their wooden skis on the shuttle before riding to the lodge. At the end of the day, a pine-lined trail allowed skiers to return back to the parking lot, an occurrence affiliated more with modern-day resorts. *Courtesy Dick Hogarth.*

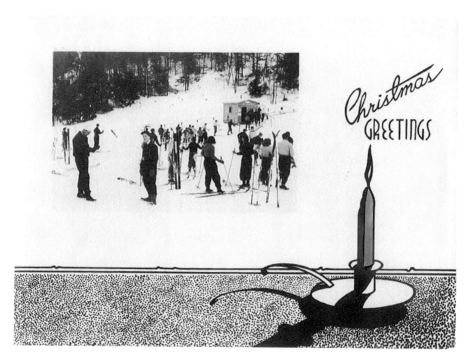

Christmas cards featuring the ski area were created for the Ski Bowl. This one shows a line of skiers waiting to use the rope tow. Charles Proctor, who designed the Sherburne Ski Trail that leads out of Tuckerman Ravine, also designed the trails reached by this rope tow. *Courtesy Dick Hogarth.*

Above: A wide-open bowl was the big feature of the ski area. The narrow trails emptied out onto this huge bowl, which funneled to the warming hut. One of the ski instructors who taught at the Ski Bowl was Jack Durrance—the brother of Dick Durrance, an accomplished ski racer. Several young skiers, including future ski area operator Bill Jenkins, used to "listen in" on Durrance's lessons in order to perfect their skiing. *Courtesy Dick Hogarth.*

Right: Ski Bowl, Inc., temporarily shut down in 1941 when Robert Hogarth took a new job managing Valley Farms in Walpole, New Hampshire. The area lay quiet until after World War II, when it was reactivated in 1946. Then managed by Edward J. Howard, Ski Bowl, Inc., occasionally had to fight off bad snow reports that announced a lack of snow when, in reality, there was enough to operate. This lift ticket is from that era. According to Howard's daughter, Ellen Howard, the ski area formally closed in February 1950 due to a lack of snow in the past season. The board of directors then sold the ski tow, equipment and buildings to Bellow Falls Village, as the land had been sold in August 1951. That ski area still operates today, with more information found in the "Survivors" chapter of this book. *Courtesy Ellen Howard.*

SUGAR BUSH

The Sugar Bush Ski Area in Jamaica began operation in the 1948–49 ski season. It was founded by Larry and Mary Weir. Larry had been an engineer with Douglas Aircraft in California, and the family had been traveling through Vermont in 1947 in order to sell an estate they had inherited before they were to move to South Africa for his job. While waiting for the area to be sold, they discovered the joys of skiing during the snowy 1947–48 ski season, decided to stay and purchased a one-hundred-acre property in Jamaica. There they cleared trails and slopes and opened the following winter with a rope tow purchased from the Guilford Street Tow in Brattleboro. A view of their Four Maple Slope is shown here. *Courtesy Tim Ingalls.*

Sugar Bush was a family-friendly ski area that catered to novices, along with having lodging available on site. The expert ski jumper Mezzy Barber from Brattleboro helped design the ski area and also taught lessons. Most trails were relatively easy, but some had a few quick drops. A portable, shorter baby tow was installed here in the early 1950s, shown here on the right in this 1953 advertisement. Skiers here were community-minded, and one day in 1952 they responded with assistance to a chimney fire at a nearby house. Once the fire was out, they returned back to their skiing! The Weirs sold the ski area in 1955, and the new owners briefly operated the area as the Mountain Brook Lodge, but the area closed only a few years later.

Chapter 5
HYBRID SKI AREAS

Some ski areas do not quite meet the definition of being fully opened or closed and thus fall somewhere in the middle. These "hybrid" areas still may offer skiing in one form or another. For example, Prospect Mountain in Woodford no longer offers lift-served downhill skiing but has an extensive cross-country trail network and maintains the land where the alpine ski area used to operate. Other areas, like Timber Ridge, do not have a traditional lift, but the trails are maintained and snowmaking occasionally occurs at this mostly private ski area.

A few areas have been merged into much larger resorts. The Gully, a rope tow area, is now a part of Suicide Six, but there is no separate lift at the formerly independent area. Carinthia was once an alternative to Mount Snow but is now the site of their terrain park area.

Another ski area was significantly lost but has now reopened as a private club. Round Top operated until the 1980s but then closed and was later fully abandoned in the 1990s. Saplings took over the ski area, and the base lodge deteriorated beyond repair. The ski area has now been completely revitalized, and a new clubhouse has been built.

At seven, the number of "hybrid" areas in southern Vermont rivals that of any other region of New England.

CARINTHIA

Carinthia Ski Area was founded in 1960 by Walter Stugger, an Austrian immigrant. Stugger had worked at other ski areas prior to opening Carinthia, including next-door Mount Snow. Seeing the popularity of Mount Snow, and knowing his own desire to build a small ski area vthe land that would become Carinthia in the late 1950s. The ski area initially offered a rope tow on a beginner's slope and a Doppelmayr T-bar for higher slopes. Plans were for many more lifts, but as seen in this 1960s plan, only lift 1 (the T-bar) and lift 2 (the rope tow) were constructed for much of the area's existence. Lift 4 would eventually be built as a double chair in 1983. *Courtesy New England Ski Museum.*

RELAX IN LUXURIOUS COMFORT

Carinthia's club house is based on the twin concepts of comfort and convenience, something quite familiar in Europe but usually neglected in the crowded commercial ski areas of the United States.

Spacious, yet intimate restaurants, both inside and on the terraces, restful lounges, well-equipped recreation rooms; a large, supervised nursery---these are the extras which will be offered in Carinthia's king-size lodge, a tasteful blend of the modern and traditional.

A fully-stocked ski shop, featuring the best in domestic and imported clothing and equipment, will be located in the ground level of the lodge, along with a quick-service repair department and storage lockers for the club members' skis.

For (after) apres-ski enjoyment there will be a setup bar, with a small dance floor.

At Carinthia skiing will be king, but none of the traditional European comforts of before and after skiing will be neglected. Weekday or weekend, there will be none of the unruly crowding and congestion or the poorly-prepared snacks hastily-gulped on littered picnic tables.

Meals will be leisurely and relaxed and there will be time and space for sunbathing or the ski-talk so essential to a pleasant winter vacation or weekend.

Carinthia Ski Club

Skiing at Carinthia was mainly for beginners and intermediates and for those who wanted to avoid the crowds of nearby Mount Snow. As Carinthia gained success, the rivalry between the two areas heated up. In order to grow, plans for condominiums, this king-sized base lodge and a Carinthia Club were developed; however, most of these plans never came to fruition. Despite this, Carinthia was seen as a viable alternative for families seeking uncrowded skiing from the 1960s into the 1980s. *Courtesy New England Ski Museum.*

Carinthia

WEST DOVER, VERMONT

In the late 1970s and early 1980s, struggles with nearby Mount Snow continued, and at one point the owners of Mount Snow had obtained use permits from the U.S. Forest Service for the land above Carinthia's T-bar. Stugger was able to get the decision reversed and was able to construct trails above the T-bar area, increasing the vertical drop from 550 feet to nearly 1,000. As the trails were not lift-served until 1983, special Sno-cats provided access, shown here as skiers descend the Upper Liftline Trail in the early 1980s. *Courtesy of the New England Ski Museum.*

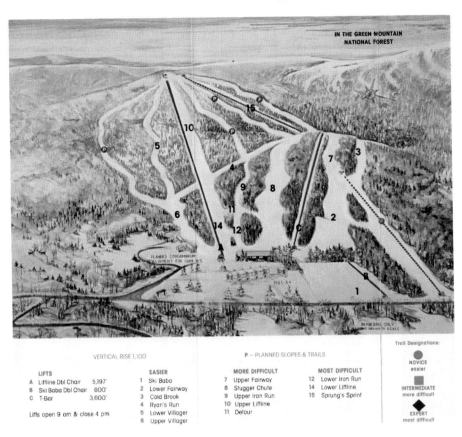

IN THE GREEN MOUNTAIN
NATIONAL FOREST

VERTICAL RISE 1,100'

P — PLANNED SLOPES & TRAILS

Trail Designations:

NOVICE
easier

INTERMEDIATE
more difficult

EXPERT
most difficult

LIFTS			EASIER		MORE DIFFICULT		MOST DIFFICULT	
A	Liftline Dbl Chair	5,197'	1	Ski Baba	7	Upper Fairway	12	Lower Iron Run
B	Ski Baba Dbl Chair	600'	2	Lower Fairway	8	Stugger Chute	14	Lower Liftline
C	T-Bar	3,600'	3	Cold Brook	9	Upper Iron Run	15	Sprung's Sprint
			4	Ryan's Run	10	Upper Liftline		
Lifts open 9 am & close 4 pm			5	Lower Villager	11	Detour		
			6	Upper Villager				

In 1983, a new Riblet Double Chair was constructed at Carinthia, expanding its vertical to nine hundred feet and providing full access to all trails. An ambitious plan to add more lifts, including one up Sprung's Sprint, was not to be. Stugger sold Carinthia to Mount Snow in 1986, which immediately connected into Carinthia. While no longer independent, Carinthia has seen major changes since being sold. In 1987, the original T-bar was replaced by the Fairway (now Heavy Metal) double chair, and the summit double was upgraded to a high-speed quad in 2007. Carinthia is now home to Mount Snow's terrain park, where it has been rated number one in the East by *Transworld*, *Ski* and *Skiing* magazines.

GLEBE MOUNTAIN FARM/TIMBER RIDGE

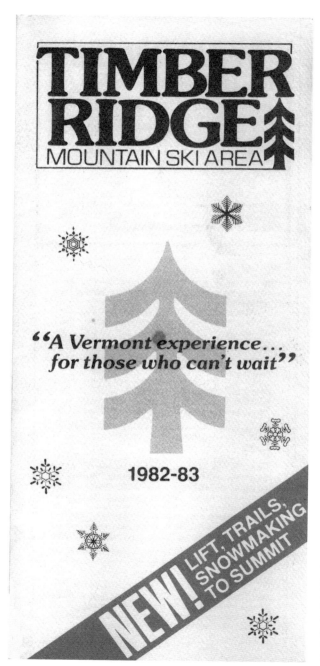

The Glebe Mountain Farm Ski Area (later Timber Ridge) in Windham was founded in 1963 by Bill Ingraham, who was associated with the Ingraham Watch Company. Initially, the ski area operated a modest T-bar and about five trails. Glebe Mountain was located on the same mountain as the Magic Mountain Ski Area. It was a semiprivate ski area that offered limited tickets to the public. Lift tickets were limited to enjoy secluded skiing.

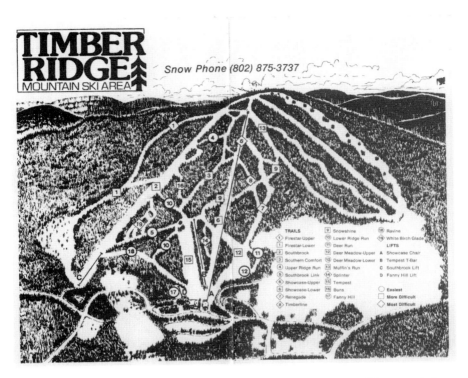

Snow Phone (802) 875-3737

TRAILS
9 Snowshine	18 Ravine
S Firestar-Upper	10 Lower Ridge Run	19 White Birch Glade
1 Firestar-Lower	11 Deer Run	LIFTS
2 Southbrook	12 Deer Meadow-Upper	A Showcase Chair
3 Southern Comfort	13 Deer Meadow-Lower	B Tempest T-Bar
4 Upper Ridge Run	14 Muffin's Run	C Southbrook Lift
5 Southbrook Link	14 Splinter	D Fanny Hill Lift
6 Showcase-Upper	15 Tempest
6 Showcase-Lower	16 Buns	○ Easiest
7 Renegade	17 Fanny Hill	□ More Difficult
8 Timberline		◇ Most Difficult

By the late 1960s, the ski area changed names to Timber Ridge and, in 1972, expanded dramatically by adding an eight-hundred-vertical-foot Hall double chair to the summit (Lift A, as shown here in this early 1980s trail map). Additional trails were cut from the summit, including the expert Renegade and easy, meandering Ridge Run Trails. Several famous actors and actresses skied here due to its private nature, including Paul Newman, Robert Redford and Grant Goodeve. Plans were drawn up in the early 1980s to expand the area even more, including a long Southbrook area with a T-bar (left) and a Glacier Bowl (right). The Glacier Bowl was never constructed, and only a short beginner's lift briefly operated at the bottom of Southbrook to ferry skiers back to the main base area.

YOU NEED THE CHALLENGE.   **YOU DESERVE THE FUN!**

This magic is no illusion. By cutting crossover trails from its 3100 foot summit, Magic linked its Magic Carpet Trail to Renegade on the Timberside of the mountain. The crossover opens twenty-five new trails to skiing for everyone from raw beginner to super star. What's more, it's easy to ski back and forth from one side of the mountain to the other. You can follow the sun, or your own sense of adventure.

There are hundreds of ways to get down Magic's big 1700-foot vertical drop. Through the glades, over the meadow, into the woods. No matter which you choose, you'll find ski terrain with real character. Beginners will love the ease and warmth of a wide sunny trail. For intermediates and experts, there's more adventure than you dare dream about in one mountain. Here you'll find trails that dart in and out of shadows; others that twist back and forth across the fall line; into and out of gaps, first narrow, then steep.

Finally there is one Eastern mountain where beginners and cruisers can choose from an array of trails designed for their own sense of excitement.

Timber Ridge struggled until the mid-1980s due to high competition. Finally, in 1987, nearby Magic Mountain purchased the ski area and connected it into their network. This created a large, multifaceted ski area with five chairlifts and two T-bars, with skiing on two faces of the mountain, as shown here in this late 1980s Magic Mountain trail map.

Lift-served skiing continued at Timber Ridge until 1991, when Magic Mountain closed temporarily. The double chair was sold to Smuggler's Notch in northern Vermont, where it operates today as Mogul Mouse's Magic Lift. In the 1990s, trails at Timber Ridge became reforested, and the base lodge was vandalized. However, in 2000, Tim Waker purchased the ski area and began to restore it. The base lodge was cleaned up and the trails brushed and cleared. A Sno-Cat was purchased to provide access to the summit, and even a small snowmaking system was installed to make terrain features. The area is mainly used by friends and family; however, a few snowboarding events have been held here. This 2008 view from the summit shows the lift foundations for the former double chair and the Showcase Slope.

Only a small portion of the ski area is visible from the base, as shown here in this March 2010 image. The double chair used to operate on Showcase (right), with the T-bar running up the line in the middle. On the left is the Tempest Slope, where snowboarding events are still held occasionally. Everything is present at this renewed ski area except a lift.

THE GULLY

The Gully was one of Woodstock's original ski areas and was founded on land owned by Mrs. Elizabeth Richmond Fisk. The Fisk family had used it as a summertime retreat. In 1935, Bunny Bertram had approached her about building a rope tow that ran on electric power, and together they opened the Gully. Bertram had a falling out with Clinton Gilbert at Gilbert's Hill at this time. The ski area was horseshoe shaped, and four rope tows were eventually installed. One of the tows was known as the "Speed Tow," which could reach eighty miles per hour! Skiing was mainly on a wide-open slope with scattered trees. Suicide Six Ski Area was begun by Bertram on the other side of the hill (Hill #6 on topographic maps) in 1937. In the mid-1950s, Suicide Six added a Pomalift, and the Gully's rope tows no longer operated. However, skiing continued at the Gully as it was merged into Suicide Six. *Courtesy Doug Riley.*

Today, the Gully is still skiable as a wide-open slope attached to the adjacent Suicide Six Ski Area. This 2005 view was taken from nearly the same location as the earlier view from the 1930s. Note that the lodge, which is still standing, is a private home today. The surrounding countryside has largely reverted back to forests. A local organization, Friends of Woodstock Winters, continues to preserve the history of Woodstock skiing and its heritage. More information can be found at www.winterfriends.org.

HITCHING POST FARM

The Hitching Post Farm rope tow was started in the 1960s by the McLaughlin family. It was primarily used as a ski camp for kids. Operating on a 750-foot-long rope tow, one slope and a few short woods trails were available. The area closed to the public in 1975. However, the area is still used privately by the family when enough snow allows for it but is not open to the public. This 2010 view shows the rope tow and wide-open slope. Today, the Hitching Post Farm is a year-round boarding and training facility dedicated to the training of horses and education of riders, according to its website at www.hitchingpostfarm.com. *Courtesy Hope McLaughlin.*

PROSPECT MOUNTAIN

Base area view

Prospect Mountain was a downhill ski area that began operation as the location of Mundell's Tow in Woodford in the late 1930s. In the late 1940s, a rope tow operated at the bottom of the future Yankee Courage Trail. However, a much larger ski area was constructed in 1960 when Bennington contractor William Morse purchased the area. He was involved with the rebuilding of Route 9, which directly passed the ski area. In the early 1960s, he installed two T-bar lifts and expanded trails to the summit, boosting its vertical to nearly 675 feet.

136

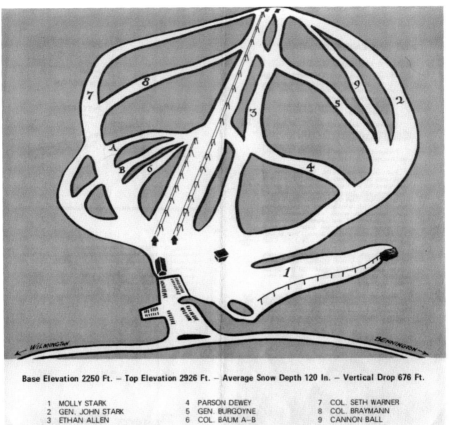

Base Elevation 2250 Ft. – Top Elevation 2926 Ft. – Average Snow Depth 120 In. – Vertical Drop 676 Ft.

1 MOLLY STARK	4 PARSON DEWEY	7 COL. SETH WARNER
2 GEN. JOHN STARK	5 GEN. BURGOYNE	8 COL. BRAYMANN
3 ETHAN ALLEN	6 COL. BAUM A–B	9 CANNON BALL

The area with a past as well as a future

If you are wondering where we got our Trail names, we refer you to your nearest library. Find a history book and turn to the period of August 16, 1777 and the Battle of Bennington.

The alpine ski area offered a wide variety of terrain, with all of the trails named after elements of the Battle of Bennington, as shown here in this 1960s trail map. The shorter T-bar allowed novice and low- to intermediate-level skiers access to the lower third of the mountain, while the beginner's rope tow served a gentle slope. The high elevation of Prospect usually resulted in higher accumulations than other lower-elevation ski areas.

As Prospect was the nearest major ski area to Bennington, many in the city learned to ski in the area. In the 1960s, an entire family could ski here for the season for less than $150! Tom Barbera, his brother Dave and his father are pictured here learning to ski on the Baby Slope in 1970. *Courtesy Tom Barbera.*

Snowmaking was never installed at Prospect, though there was usually enough snow, particularly in the 1960s and early 1970s. Tom and Dave Barbera are pictured here on the John Stark Trail enjoying some fresh snowfall. By the mid- to late 1970s, Prospect began to slip, with some poor snow years and increasing competition taking their toll. The area was not making a profit. In 1978, Joe Parks purchased Prospect from Morse and began to improve the area. He invested $500,000 into Prospect, upgrading the lifts and buildings. Unfortunately, the timing could not have been worse, with two nearly snowless seasons to follow in 1979 and 1980. *Courtesy Tom Barbera.*

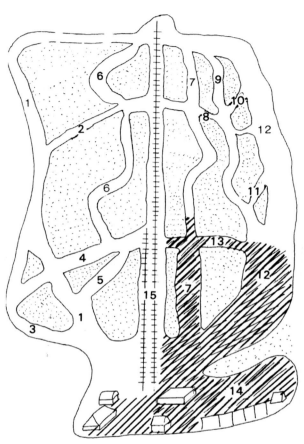

Legend

#	NAME	ABILITY
1	Seth Warner	Easiest
2	Redcoat Run	Easiest
3	Smoothbore	Easiest
4	Independence	Easiest
5	Baum's Run	Expert
6	Ticonderoga Glade	Expert
7	Yankee Courage	Expert
8	Grenadier	Easiest
9	Cannon Ball	Expert
10	Dragoon	Easiest
11	Flintlock	Intermediate
12	John Stark	Intermediate
13	Powderhorn	Easiest
14	Baby Slope	Easiest
15	T-Bar Lifts	No Skiing

NIGHT SKIING

Poor snow seasons continued into the 1980s, and the focus gradually turned away from the alpine ski area to the Prospect Mountain Ski Touring Center, which was built by Joe Parks. The cross-country trails required less snow to open. Cross-country skiers could also ride up the alpine T-bar to the summit, where several cross-country trails were available. This 1982 trail map shows the alpine ski area as it would remain for the next ten years. Nighttime skiing was available on the lower slopes on Friday nights; the downhill ski area operated on Friday afternoons, holidays and weekends.

Joe Parks continued to own and operate the ski area until 1990, when it was sold. However, the downhill ski area only operated until 1991, when it was closed for good. This late 1980s view of the T-bars shows the bottom of the ski area late in its operation. *Courtesy John Hitchcock.*

Today, Prospect Mountain no longer offers lift-served alpine skiing; however, it remains a thriving cross-country ski center owned by Steve Whitham. Some trails meander through the former alpine ski area. Its high elevation and high annual snowfalls allow for some of the earliest and latest cross-country skiing available in southern Vermont and New England. For more information, visit www.prospectmountain.com. This November 2009 view of the parking lot shows the two T-bars on the left and the Ethan Allen Trail on the right. All alpine trails are still very well maintained.

ROUND TOP—BEAR CREEK CLUB

Big league skiing with friendly people
5 miles south of Killington Gondola,
Route 100, Plymouth, Vermont, 05056

Round Top Ski Area was founded in 1964 by Paul Goldman. It was a medium-sized ski area with a 1,200-foot vertical drop and was a favorite of families who wanted to avoid the crowds at nearby Killington. Built on Salt Ash Mountain, the ski area featured beautiful views of the surrounding area and had fifteen trails. A three-level base lodge, built to resemble a barn, served skiers at its base.

A Salt Ash Chair (4600')
B Boulder Chair (3100')
C Tinker T-Bar (1000')
D Handletow (400')
E Base Lodge
F Nursery
G Ski School Meeting Place
H Patrol & First Aid Room

● Easiest ■ More difficult ◆ Most difficult

1 Goldbrook ■	4 Mogulch ■	7 Upper Salt Ash ◆	10 Chute ●	13 Balancing Rock ■
2 Roller Coaster ■	5 Tinker ●	8 Lower Salt Ash ■	11 Woodpecker ◆	14 Glades ■
3 Coolidge ◆	6 Pushover ●	9 Route 100 ●	12 Boulder Bowl ■	15 Wedel Village ●

Our PSIA-Member Ski School has been developed with the goal of building a staff of dedicated professionals. Outstanding teaching ability, a warm personality, and a love of skiing are the qualities that make each instructor capable of teaching all ages and levels of ability.

Our aim is to teach you how to have fun, be safe on skis, and, at the same time, learn how to ski well. Whether you have a weekend, a week, or a season to improve your skiing abilities, your learning experience will not be better guided anywhere in the East.

Class lessons are 1½ hour sessions. Before each class you are carefully placed with a group on the terrain of your ability, and classes are constantly monitored so that you will be quickly promoted to another class if you excell, and no time is wasted.

If you have a week to spend, you will have time to develop a real rapport with our instructors in daily lessons, free skiing, informal afternoon get-togethers with instructors in the lodge

and closing festivities at week's end.

Seasonal programs in freestyle and racing are designed for all ages. Juniors 18 and under can qualify for teams which compete to represent Round Top in competitions at other New England ski areas.

Multi-Day Ski Vacations. Start any day, stay as long as you like. Special prices for any number of days, any combination of skiing, instruction, rentals, nursery, and lodging. Rental equipment for all teaching methods available. Daily lessons continue with personalized attention from our instructors in the lodge after skiing.

Snowmaking assures best possible conditions.

Ladies (Thurs.) and Men's (Wed.) Days. All day, all area lift ticket—plus 1½ hour class lesson plus complete rental equipment—all for only a couple of dollars more than a lift ticket alone! Special nursery rates for ladies on Thursdays. Inquire about our new 8-session series.

Above: Access to the summit was provided by the Salt Ash Double Chair, installed in 1964 when the ski area was founded. A shorter Boulder Double Chair was constructed in 1968 to relieve pressure off the summit lift. Beginners used the original Tinker T-bar or the Handle Tow to learn how to ski. A wide variety of skiing was available at Round Top, from the twisty Roller Coaster Trail to the steep Coolidge Trail, named after President Coolidge, who was born and took the presidential oath of office just a few miles away. This trail map dates from the late 1970s, which was the peak of skiing at Round Top.

Opposite top: As a medium-sized independent ski area surrounded by larger mountains, Round Top struggled against the competition in the 1970s and early 1980s. Bankruptcy was declared in 1974; however, Paul Goldman's son, David, purchased the area and operated it until 1981. A small snowmaking system was installed in 1977, along the Boulder Trail and Wedel Village, up to the summit. However, the snowmaking improvements were not enough for the ski area to succeed. The area declared bankruptcy again in 1981 and closed in 1982. This view shows the Salt Ash Chair and Salt Ash Slope in the 1960s.

Round Top was then closed from 1982 until 1997. Like all lost ski areas, nature took over quickly, and saplings grew on the slopes. In 1988, the State of Vermont ordered a cleanup of the underground oil and gasoline tanks that had begun to spill. After it was cleaned up, Round Top continued to return to nature, as shown here in 1996 just prior to the rebirth of the ski area. *Courtesy David Dematteis.*

After being closed for nearly fifteen years, Round Top was reborn in 1997 as the Bear Creek Club. Founders David Yurkerwich and John Neal invested in and redeveloped the ski area and base facilities, refurbishing the double chair to the top and building a brand-new clubhouse. The ski area is run as a private club, and more information can be viewed at www.bearcreekclub.com. This 2005 view of the double chair and Upper Salt Ash Trail show how uncrowded the skiing is, with plenty of light powder that day.

SONNENBERG/TWIN FARMS

Sonnenberg Ski Area, the "Sun Mountain," was founded in 1967 by Mr. and Mrs. Hans Kurash. Kurash was a construction executive from Philadelphia and had purchased Twin Farms, which was the retreat of Sinclair Lewis and Dorothy Thompson in Barnard. Two lifts were installed in 1967: a nondetachable summit Pomalift as well as a beginner's Pomalift. Several trails were served by these lifts on a nearly four-hundred-foot vertical drop. Then, in 1974, a family corporation owned by the Twigg-Smith family purchased the ski area and surrounding property. Thurston "Koke" and Andrea "Andi" Twigg-Smith operated the ski area. Pictured here is their son, Jason, in 1983 on the ski area's "Jump Trail," which was full of jumps and was essentially Vermont's first terrain park. *Courtesy Koke Twigg-Smith.*

Above: Like many small ski areas, most everybody knew each other, and the employees and ski patrol were like family. Everybody worked hard to keep the ski area operating. Sonnenberg tried out several techniques to be competitive in a tough ski market. Most ski areas in the 1980s prohibited the new sport of snowboarding; however, Sonnenberg embraced it. In fact, the Twigg-Smiths' other son, Kina, as well as ski patroller Jim Hudson, became the first snowboarding members of the national ski patrol. Pictured here are the staff and patrollers at Sonnenberg in 1987. Standing right to left are sons Jason and Kina, as well as Andi and Koke Twigg-Smith. *Courtesy Koke Twigg-Smith.*

Opposite top: As a small ski area, Sonnenberg faced strong competition. Snowmaking was too expensive to be installed, and some poor snow years in the '80s contributed to its eventual closure as a public ski area. In the late 1980s, Sonnenberg attempted to survive by becoming an exclusive ski area, with the most expensive ticket in the country priced at forty five dollars. This included uncrowded skiing and a gourmet lunch. Sadly, this did not work out, and the area was turned back into Twin Farms, a private inn that offered skiing for guests in 1991. Twin Farms would remain in the family until 2004, when it was sold. This view of the slopes of Twin Farms was taken in 2010. *Courtesy Hope McLaughlin.*

Opposite bottom: Today, Twin Farms is a highly rated, exclusive and private resort, and skiing is not available to the public. As of recently, the lift no longer operates; however, the resort maintains the ski area with well-groomed trails and access by Sno-Cat to the summit for guests of the resort only. For more information about Twin Farms, visit www.twinfarms. com. A few relics of the Sonnenberg days remain, such as this writing on a building on the slopes in 2010. *Courtesy Hope McLaughlin.*

Chapter 6
THE SURVIVORS

The loss of sixty ski areas in southern Vermont has left the area with far fewer choices to ski. Almost all of the family- and community-style ski areas have been lost. Victims of poor snowfalls, competition, changing skier habits and bad luck, these areas will be remembered fondly by all those who skied them. The major resorts today offer some incredible experiences but can often lack the intimacy at these smaller areas.

However, two small ski areas have managed to survive for many years and offer the skier a chance to experience what skiing was like decades ago. Living Memorial Park in Brattleboro is an all-volunteer-run location with downhill skiing and snowboarding, a small terrain park, snowmaking and a T-bar lift. Though small, the ski area is thriving and receives good community support.

The last publicly availably rope tow ski area continues to operate in Bellows Falls at Rockingham Recreation. This area features a speedy rope tow, a wide-open slope and trail and a warming hut. If you want to experience an old-fashioned ski area, this is the place.

At the time of this writing, both Rockingham Recreation and Living Memorial Park offer five-dollar lift tickets—just 6 percent of what it would cost at one of the larger resorts.

It is doubtful that any other small ski area may return to operation, but it is not impossible. With strong community support and good financial support, anything is possible.

LIVING MEMORIAL PARK

Living Memorial Park operates as a family-friendly ski area in Brattleboro. It began as the Guilford Street Tow in the 1930s and 1940s, briefly closed once its tow was sold to the Sugar Bush Ski Area in Jamaica and was then reopened by the Rotary Club in the 1950s. In 1965, the town replaced the rope tow with a T-bar. The ski area continued to operate until 1995, when a poor snow year resulted in its closure. However, in 1997, a nonprofit group—Living Memorial Park Snow Sports, Inc.—was formed to reopen the ski area, which it did in 1999. Today, the ski area features two slopes, one of which has an introductory terrain park. Here, skiers and snowboarders ride the T-bar to the summit of this two-hundred-foot vertical hill.

The ski area is completely volunteer-run and is very popular with residents of Brattleboro. Volunteers were able to install a small snowmaking system to ensure skiing when the weather doesn't cooperate. Often, students from the local high school help run the lifts as part of their community service requirement. The ski area is open on weekends and on Thursday and Friday nights under the lights and features a terrific view, as shown here. As of 2010, lift tickets were only five dollars. Living Memorial Park is a great example of how a small ski area with the right community support can still thrive in our modern era. For more information on the ski area, visit www.vtsnowsports.org. *Courtesy Paul Lemieux.*

ROCKINGHAM RECREATION ROPE TOW

The Rockingham Recreation Department operates southern Vermont's last publicly operated rope tow ski area. Founded in 1953 by the Town of Rockingham and the Village of Bellows Falls, it utilized the rope tow that formerly operated at Ski Bowl, Inc., in nearby Saxton's River. It features a wide-open, moderately steep slope and a woods trail, all served by a 950-foot-long rope tow. It is staffed by volunteers and is open most weekends. A small warming hut with snacks is available, shown here at the base of the tow, donated by Ben and Jerry's.

A beautiful view of Bellows Falls and nearby hills in New Hampshire greet skiers at the top of the rope tow. The skiing here is simple and uncrowded and is the last example of what skiing was like decades ago at a town rope tow ski area. Lift tickets are very affordable; in 2010, they were just five dollars for a day of skiing. For more information, visit the town's website at www.rockbf.org.

CONCLUSION

Although so many ski areas have vanished in southern Vermont, the remaining ski areas offer tremendous skiing that is popular across the Northeast and even around the world. Most resorts such as Stratton, Mount Snow and Killington offer high-speed quad chairlifts, large vertical drops and plenty of trails. Besides the surviving community ski areas, old-fashioned skiing can still be found at Magic Mountain and at Pico. Medium-sized Suicide Six and the semiprivate Quechee Lakes offer family skiing on a decent variety of trails and slopes.

It appears that the huge loss of the number of operating ski areas has come to an end. The past few years have seen few closings, and some small areas such as Living Memorial Park have become revitalized. Southern Vermont has reached a sort of equilibrium, and it is hoped that all remaining ski areas will thrive in the next decade. Supporting these smaller ski areas is vital to their continued role of teaching the next generation to love the sport.

If you remember skiing or working at any of these lost ski areas, now is the time to preserve your memories and photographs. You can submit any information to the New England Lost Ski Areas Project website, at www.nelsap.org. Here you can learn more about the former ski areas across New England and read additional memories of areas in southern Vermont.

Two terrific museums deal specifically with ski history and are an excellent starting point if you would like to learn more on the subject. The New England Ski Museum (www.skimuseum.org), located in Franconia Notch, New Hampshire, documents ski history from around New England and the world. The Vermont Ski Museum (www.vermontskimuseum.org) in Stowe, Vermont, has wonderful exhibits on ski history in the state, including lost ski areas. If you like ski history, it is strongly recommended that you join these organizations and support their efforts.

ABOUT THE AUTHOR

Jeremy Davis grew up in Chelmsford, Massachusetts, and learned to ski at Nashoba Valley. In the 1990s, he skied frequently in southern Vermont and began to explore the lost ski areas in that region. He founded the New England Lost Ski Areas Project (www.nelsap.org) in 1998 and graduated from Lyndon State College in Lyndonville, Vermont, in 2000 with a degree in meteorology. He has served on the board of directors of the New England Ski Museum since 2000 and is employed as a senior meteorologist at Weather Routing Inc. He is also the author of *Lost Ski Areas of the*  *White Mountains*. Residing in Saratoga Springs, New York, Davis remains a frequent skier in southern Vermont today.